T0326361

The Cat Has Nine Lives

German Film Classics

Series Editors

Gerd Gemünden, Dartmouth College
Johannes von Moltke, University of Michigan

Advising Editors

Anton Kaes, University of California-Berkeley
Eric Rentschler, Harvard University

Editorial Board

Hester Baer, University of Maryland
Mattias Frey, University of Kent
Rembert Hüser, Goethe University, Frankfurt
Claudia Lenssen, Journalist and Film Critic, Berlin
Cristina Nord, Berlinale Forum
Brad Prager, University of Missouri
Reinhild Steingröver, Eastman School of Music

Also in the series:

THE CAT HAS NINE LIVES

HESTER BAER

 CAMDEN HOUSE

First published 2022 by Camden House

Camden House is an imprint of Boydell & Brewer Inc.
668 Mt. Hope Avenue, Rochester, NY 14620, USA
and of Boydell & Brewer Limited
PO Box 9, Woodbridge, Suffolk IP12 3DF, UK
www.boydellandbrewer.com

Cover image: The eroticization of plant life. Screenshot from *The Cat Has Nine Lives*. Courtesy of Stiftung Deutsche Kinemathek.

ISBN-13: 978-1-64014-099-8

Library of Congress Cataloging-in-Publication Data

CIP data is available from the Library of Congress.

This publication is printed on acid-free paper.
Printed in the United States of America.

Publication of this book was supported by a grant from the German Film Institute (GFI) of the University of Michigan Department of Germanic Languages & Literatures.

CONTENTS

ACKNOWLEDGMENTS

The Cat Has Nine Lives presages a feminist future that is yet to come even as it archives a past that has been foreclosed upon. Encountering this 1968 film following its rerelease in 2019, I was most struck by the sense of suspended time that it engenders: it resonates anew with conversations about feminist film and media in the twenty-first century while also revivifying a previous moment of aesthetic and political potential that contrasts sharply with the impasse of the neoliberal present. Deferred timelines also characterize the reception history of Ula Stöckl's film, which is not as well known as it should be, especially to Anglophone viewers, partly because it failed to find a distributor after its premiere. This book seeks to restore *The Cat Has Nine Lives*, the first West German feminist film, to its rightful place as a German film classic.

I am grateful to Ula Stöckl for her generosity in speaking with me at length about *Nine Lives* and her other films. Those conversations would not have been possible without Angelica Fenner. My thinking about Stöckl's oeuvre emerged in dialogue with Angelica, and this book is very much a product of our ongoing collaboration. The conference that Angelica organized at the University of Toronto in 2019, "From Feminist Filmmaking to Pro Quote Film: Historicizing Authorship, Gender, and Performance in 21st-Century German Cinema," provided the initial impetus for this project. I thank her and all the participants at the conference, especially Barbara Mennel and Jeanne Richter, for their inspiring comments and discussions. My gratitude also goes to series editors Gerd Gemünden and Johannes von Moltke and to Camden House editorial director Jim Walker for their enthusiasm about the project and for the generous feedback that they and the anonymous reviewer provided on the manuscript. Thank you to Phil Dematteis for his meticulous and instructive copyediting and to Jane Best for her care with the book's production.

Diana Kluge and Julia Riedel at the Stiftung Deutsche Kinemathek in Berlin provided valuable assistance and guidance.

The deferred temporalities that characterize *The Cat Has Nine Lives* were mirrored by the strange, simultaneous expansion and compression of time that I experienced while working on this book, which was conceived of just prior to the coronavirus pandemic and written in its entirety during the lockdown, when libraries and archives were closed. I am immensely grateful to University of Maryland librarian Jordan Sly, who worked miracles in helping me gain access to research materials despite the closure. Presenting part of the manuscript in progress at the 2020 virtual conference of the Coalition of Women in German helped me to clarify aspects of my analysis; I thank Amy Lynne Hill and Faye Stewart for organizing the panel "Slutty Sluts who Slut: Promiscuity and Sexuality through the Ages." Thank you to my parents, Clint and Elizabeth Baer, for their ongoing support and for offering me the use of their apartment for a writing retreat where I finished the manuscript. I am profoundly lucky to have shared the time and space of quarantine with Della Baer and Ryan Long, whose humor, creativity, wisdom, dance parties, and shared TikTok videos provided daily inspiration. If it's true that "for three she plays, for three she strays, for three she stays," then I'm grateful that Rosie the Cat must be living the latter third of her nine lives, making her a loyal writing companion.

The Cat Has Nine Lives

In the Driver's Seat

A woman sits at the wheel. From her perspective, we see the road ahead. Placed in the center of the frame, the car's rearview mirror reflects the driver's face as she watches the road and then glances directly into the mirror, creating a relay of looks back to the camera and the audience (fig. 1). The fact that the woman is wearing glasses emphasizes her active gaze throughout this opening sequence as she maneuvers her car through city traffic. Moving fluidly between over-the-shoulder interior shots and external views of the car taken from multiple angles, the camera figures the mobility of identity, desire, and social position that the five women protagonists of *The Cat Has Nine Lives* (*Neun Leben hat die Katze*, 1968)—including the driver, Katharina—pursue.

With these opening images, director Ula Stöckl offers a striking critique of the heteropatriarchal looking relations that underpin

Figure 1. Katharina (Liane Hielscher) initiates a relay of looks back to the camera and the audience.

dominant cinema, five years before feminist film critic Laura Mulvey first formulated her reading of the male gaze. Memorably summarized by the dictum "woman as image, man as bearer of the look," Mulvey's groundbreaking analysis examines how film "reflects, reveals, and even plays on the straight, socially established interpretation of sexual difference which controls images, erotic ways of looking and spectacle."[1] Depicting Katharina as both de-eroticized image and active bearer of the look, the opening sequence of *Nine Lives* deconstructs conventional modes of representing women on-screen and draws attention to structures of looking; as such, it offers a preview of the film's broader exploration of feminist aesthetics and women's emancipation at the key historical turning point of 1968.

Katharina (Liane Hielscher) is driving to the train station where she will meet her French friend, Anne (Kristine de Loup), who arrives in Munich from Paris for an extended visit. The two women seem to be opposites: Katharina seeks purpose and independence through work—she hopes to make it as a freelance journalist—while Anne works only to pay the rent, finding meaning not in professional life but through human interaction, encounters with the natural world, and making things. Despite these ostensible differences, however, what Katharina and Anne share in common is a quest for self-determination as they attempt to break out of the preordained roles that have constrained previous generations of women.

Posing the question, "Women have never had as many possibilities to do what they want as they have today, but do they know what they want?," *Nine Lives* imaginatively visualizes changing constellations of gender and sexuality, confounding both gender norms and cinematic conventions to envision social and aesthetic change. The film examines the question of desire and self-determination through five characters, all of whom embody different aspects of women's experience, subjectivity, and fantasy. The friends Katharina and Anne are the most developed of the five characters, and they offer two distinctive pathways toward emancipation, but each of the other three central figures allows us to engage with a different facet of womanhood.

The only mother among the five women, Magdalena (Elke Kummer), the wife of Katharina's lover Stefan, is a homemaker raising two young sons. Magdalena conforms most closely to traditional expectations for women, but she is also portrayed in several of the film's fantasy sequences pointing a gun at her husband, Stefan's, head, suggesting how the violence of women's domestic confinement incites further violence.

Pop singer Gabriele (Heidi Stroh), whom Katharina interviews for a magazine profile, balances her ambition for success in a male-dominated industry with her ambivalence about the sexual objectification that is the price of celebrity. An extended sequence depicts Gabriele's creative process as she works with various (male) collaborators to write and record the song "The Cat Has Nine Lives." Observed by Katharina, this sequence offers a self-reflective take—underscored by the fact that Stöckl's film shares its title with Gabriele's song—on women's authorship and on the predicament of artists (including both pop singers and filmmakers) working within the confines of a culture industry whose dominant conventions limit imagination and creativity.

Meanwhile, appearances by Kirke (Antje Ellermann), based on Circe, the witch from Greek mythology who notably turned men into swine, punctuate *Nine Lives*. A figment of protagonist Anne's imagination or perhaps her alter ego, Kirke explicitly defies gender and sexual norms. Identified in the screenplay as "a sorceress with a fine lady's mustache," this gender nonconforming character draws particular attention to the ways that femininity and women's desire are policed in dominant society.[2] Anne describes Kirke as a nymphomaniac, a monomaniac, and a kleptomaniac who is "sometimes" married and who does exactly what she wants. Like her namesake, she turns men—including, in one scene, the entire film crew of *Nine Lives*—into pigs, and she also initiates erotic interactions in ways that remain difficult for the women in the film who exist outside the realm of fantasy.

The magical Kirke brings into focus the theme of sexual liberation, a key horizon for the film and one that connects all of its women characters. Although Katharina, Anne, Magdalena, and Gabriele occupy a range of sexual positionalities, they all struggle to break with normative expectations, which are defined by the heteropatriarchal institution of marriage. Devotedly promiscuous, Katharina pursues a love affair with the married Stefan (Jürgen Arndt), a nonmonogamous arrangement that she prefers because it facilitates her own sexual autonomy and allows her to sleep with whomever she wishes. A character who might today be understood as polyamorous, Katharina vocally advocates for antirepressive sex education: in one scene, she visits a day care, where she encourages children to place pillows between their legs and ride them like horses. Noting that she herself had been shamed and punished by her parents when she was discovered pleasuring herself as a child, she points out that fostering autoeroticism is important because it enables independence from any partner.

Recently divorced, Anne likewise questions the link between sexuality and love and its implications for women's emancipation from prescribed roles. Calling attention to the hypocritical ways in which men manipulate women sexually through amorous promises, Anne asks every man she kisses, "Do you love me?," but she ultimately chooses none of them. Anne is vocally critical of the extramarital affair between Katharina and Stefan: she repeatedly refers to Katharina as "Stefanie." By labeling her friend with the feminine version of the name Stefan, Anne pokes fun at Katharina's attempt to emancipate herself from sexual norms by compromising another woman's marriage, expressing through irony her concern about what she views as an unethical relation.

As Katharina drives to the train station to meet Anne in the opening sequence of *Nine Lives*, a song begins to play. This chanson,

"Fleurs de Vacances" (Vacation Flowers), by the actor who plays Anne, Kristine de Loup, introduces two crucial motifs of the film: language and flowers.[3] Sung in French, the chanson signals the multilingualism of *Nine Lives*, which constantly vacillates between French and German and places an emphasis on code-switching and wordplay, elements that disrupt and satirize the gendering of linguistic norms and also denaturalize links between language and national identity, enabling a critical approach to Germanness.

The song's repeated lyric "Je serai la fleur de vos vacances" (I will be the flower of your vacation) figures the metonymic link—one of the most striking of this visually inventive film—between the vacationing Anne and plant life, especially flowers. This association, first invoked by the music, is repeated visually when Katharina arrives at the train station. A tracking shot unspools a view of a busy shopping arcade, before a cut focuses our attention on one shop in particular, whose sign reads "Süsswaren Blumen" (candy and flowers). A medium close-up shows women buying and selling flowers, and we see Katharina purchasing a yellow rose. Here, the chanson ends, and a shift to diegetic sound accompanies a visual transition to the space of the train station. Anne disembarks from the train, and Katharina presents her with the rose.

In the course of *Nine Lives*, we will see Anne clothe herself in floral prints and jewelry, place fresh blossoms in her hair, craft paper flowers and later set them on fire, draw botanical motifs on her skin, and repeatedly lick and eat blooms. Pictured in the saturated reds and greens of Technicolor, floral images literally garland the film, contributing to its visual pleasures (figs. 2a–c). But Anne's association with flowers also forms a key vector for the film's critical reflection on the decorative role of women in dominant cinema, which Mulvey famously termed "to-be-looked-at-ness" (19). This association likewise facilitates the film's broader critique of women's position in patriarchal society, which the German film critic Frieda Grafe refers to, in a 1974 review of Stöckl's film, as the floral quality

Figures 2a–c. Floral images garland *The Cat Has Nine Lives.*

of women ("weibliche Blumenhaftigkeit").⁴ Ultimately, Anne's play
with the vegetal presents a site of fantasy—linked to the dream

sequences, surreal vignettes, traumatic flashbacks, and hallucinatory images punctuating the film—that is crucial to the utopian vision Stöckl unfolds.

In her review, Grafe describes the predicament of the woman artist: "How can women say what kind of world they wish for, when their existence is defined by a fundamental muteness, because someone was always there before them and so nothing is left for them but perpetually to react [to what came before?]" (101). Katharina herself describes this dilemma later in one of the film's fantasy scenes, when her voice-over intones, "We can only ever imagine what already exists." Responding to this conundrum, Stöckl sought not only to undo the conventions that had shaped women's representation on-screen but to begin the process of envisioning an alternative cinematic imaginary.

First Feminist Film

The Cat Has Nine Lives premiered at the Mannheim Film Festival on October 12, 1968. Its premiere coincided with the birth of second-wave feminism in postwar Germany, which is generally attributed to a speech presented by Helke Sander on behalf of the Action Council for the Liberation of Women at a meeting of the Socialist German Student Organization (Sozialistischer Deutscher Studentenbund, SDS) just one month earlier, in September 1968. Sander, herself a film student in Berlin at the time, would go on to become one of the most significant feminist filmmakers in West Germany. As an activist for women's participation in filmmaking, Sander helped to facilitate the emergence of the West German feminist film project, which began to consolidate in 1973 and celebrated its first well-known features, including Sander's own *The All-Around Reduced Personality* (*Die allseitig reduzierte Persönlichkeit*)—also known by the acronym *Redupers*—in 1977.

Subsequently recognized as postwar Germany's very first feminist film, *Nine Lives* anticipates the concerns of both the emergent women's movement and the feminist film project, neither of which yet existed as such when the film premiered in Mannheim.[5] Debuting in advance of later developments that might have helped to contextualize it, Stöckl's film elaborates a radical aesthetics and politics of women's (sexual) liberation that could not be assimilated in the 1960s, a fact that helps to explain the film's widespread indictment by contemporary viewers and critics.[6] Audiences in Mannheim, comprised largely of students, demanded that the festival prize money should not be awarded to any of the films on view but instead used to donate bicycles to Vietnam. *Nine Lives* was singled out for particular criticism because it was perceived as apolitical owing to its focus on the so-called secondary contradiction (*Nebenwiderspruch*) of women's subjugation—rather than the primary contradiction produced by capitalism, class difference—and because of its pop style.

Plagued by this negative reception, *Nine Lives* disappeared from view shortly after its 1968 premiere following the bankruptcy of its distributor Eckelkamp, which had been set to debut the film in six thousand West German cinemas.[7] Stöckl's attempt to locate a different distributor for the film failed. Notably, when she approached the distribution company Ceres-Film, they offered her a contract on the condition that Stöckl add several explicitly pornographic scenes to *Nine Lives* that would allow it to be distributed as a sex film, an offer that underscores how the film's defiance of classical cinematic depictions of women made it legible only as smut in the Federal Republic of 1968. Ultimately, *Nine Lives* never debuted in cinemas; its limited exhibition and reception at the time is one reason why the film has remained relatively unknown to audiences ever since.

In the twenty-first century, however, interest in women's film-making has experienced a resurgence. The fiftieth anniversary of 1968 revitalized attention to the events and cultural movements of this revolutionary year and to the paths not taken in its aftermath. Meanwhile, the hashtag campaigns #TimesUp and #MeToo raised new awareness of the underrepresentation of women and widespread sexism in the global film and media industries. Activist organizations, including the German feminist group Pro Quote Film (PQF; For a Film Quota), have sought to address this situation by promoting a quota system to establish equitable funding and staffing in film and television. These developments have driven a renewed focus on the historical legacies of feminist cinema, including the significant place of *Nine Lives* in film history. Stöckl's film was revived at the Berlin Film Festival in 2019 as part of the retrospective "Self-Determined: Perspectives of Women Filmmakers" and subsequently released on DVD for the first time, in a restored version with English subtitles.[8]

Nine Lives presents an important aesthetic and political precursor to the cinefeminism of later decades, but as several critics have suggested, it is perhaps equally noteworthy for offering provocations that were not widely taken up by feminist filmmaking in the 1970s and 1980s. For instance, actor and critic Toby Ashraf finds queer traces in *Nine Lives*, which, like Stöckl's other films, offers "radical, other models of relationships, sexuality, and identity" that defy normative categories. Writer and director Tatjana Turanskyj, one of the founders of PQF, praises the process-based, "cut-up-style narrative form" of the film, which enables its complex depiction of women's diverse biographies and its simultaneous critique of the conditions in which they develop.[9] Indeed, these two dimensions of *Nine Lives* are interrelated, as the film's nonlinear, episodic narrative style figures its disruption, or queering, of conventional modes of depicting gender and sexuality on screen.

After Katharina meets Anne at the train station, we see the two women seated at an outdoor café. Their conversation, which introduces the oblique manner in which characters communicate throughout *Nine Lives*, is disjunctive, but it circuitously initiates the film's critical discourse on women's self-determination and the institution of marriage. Anne prompts Katharina to tell her about her work. "Oh, my work," replies Katharina, "It's going well. A bit tiresome, but that's normal, right?"[10] "And Stefan?" Anne asks. Here, a cutaway from the women shows a black flag waving in the wind, a harbinger of the distress we subsequently see on Katharina's face as she imagines someone telling Stefan's wife that he is having an affair. Again, the camera cuts away to a series of seemingly unrelated images; only subsequently will we realize that this is Stefan's wife pointing a gun at his head—a vision of how Magdalena would react to learning about her husband's betrayal. Next we see Anne, now costumed differently, in a blue dress and white sun hat festooned with fresh flowers. In voice-over, she speaks in French: "I really can't tell Katharina now that I got divorced." A long shot portrays Anne and a man standing on opposite sides of a river in a visualization of their separation. Shortly afterward, when Anne asks her whether she would marry Stefan, Katharina's response emphasizes that the institution of marriage represents an impasse for her: "I can't say. I don't think divorce is a solution. Nor is marriage, actually." Anne tells Katharina that she is tired, and they leave the café, returning to Katharina's apartment, where they climb into bed together. Although not overtly eroticized, the women's easy physical intimacy as they snuggle and laugh together in bed offers a counterpoint to the confrontational depiction of their relationships with men in the opening sequence. Throughout the film, the two friends will share such moments of intimacy in ways that suggest the possibility of desire emerging between them.

When they wake up, Katharina works at the kitchen table, consulting several thick books as she types an article she is writing. Meanwhile, Anne, who is smoking, begins to tear at her pantyhose and then burn small holes in them with her cigarette (fig. 3). The action of ruining her hose, like the apocryphal bra burnings of second-wave feminism, suggests a small rebellion against the beauty standards that govern women's lives. Appealing to multisensory

Figure 3. Haptic visuality: Anne (Kristine de Loup) pokes holes in beauty standards.

experiences of touch and smell, these vivid images of ripped and melting nylon, and of Anne's skin underneath it, further call attention to the film's broader focus on women's embodiment and bodily vulnerability. Here and elsewhere, *Nine Lives* offers a mode of viewing that resonates with what film scholar Laura U. Marks has called "haptic visuality," where "the eyes themselves function like organs of touch."[11] As Marks explains, this mode of viewing appeals to nonvisual and embodied forms of knowledge and "conceives of knowledge as something gained not on the model of vision but through physical contact" (138). By emphasizing senses that film is technically unable to represent, scenes such as this one probe the limits of sight and sound, forging tactile connections to bodies and objects on screen and offering a critical take on dominant regimes of vision.

As she continues to play with fire, Anne's (self-)destruction escalates to the point where she sets a whole matchbook on fire, and the blaze that ensues startles her out of her reverie. A smash cut initiates a new scene, where Anne, Katharina, and Stefan sit together at an outdoor café. While Anne sits on Katharina's lap, Stefan tries to teach the Frenchwoman to pronounce the "H" sound at the start of "Heiliger Georg." St. George, the biblical dragon slayer, fascinates

Anne, and representations of this saint and his horse—symbolic for the victory of good over evil—reappear several times throughout the film. Anne comments on the beauty of their surroundings, and the camera pans across the pastoral lakeside landscape as she repeats a sentiment that she first uttered in the earlier café scene with Katharina: "Beauty always makes me sad." This statement provides a segue to one of the film's most iconic fantasy sequences. Anne, dressed in a white turtleneck and white jeans, appears immersed in white flowers (fig. 4). As nondiegetic music plays, she floats in a rowboat on the lake, surrounded by branches covered in blooms. Anne exits the boat, and then fills it with flowering branches; in another shot, she plucks blossoms from the branches and drops them overboard into the water. Finally, we see Anne herself floating in the water, fully clothed, dissonant music playing as her body submerges. The scene shifts to a dark hallway. Wearing a white dress, Anne advances toward the camera; we hear her voice pronouncing the words "The last time I died . . .," a kind of caption for this entire sequence. A reverse shot confirms that we are witnessing a wedding: Anne is shot from behind, taking the hand of a man in a black suit. Overtly equating marriage with women's death, this sequence encapsulates the critical take on heteronormative institutions, and the role of

Figure 4. The floral quality of women: Anne surrounds herself with flowers.

beauty in sustaining them, that is developed throughout the opening of *Nine Lives*. As Grafe describes it, "The beauty that we women are tasked with bringing to the lives of men is abundantly evident in Ula Stöckl's work. Flowers, flowers, flowers. People as flowers, images as flowers, flowers as flowers."[12]

Within the diegetic narrative, Anne seeks to expose how Stefan treats women precisely as such decorative ornaments to surround himself with. Seated at a restaurant, she asks him, "Do you love Katharina?" Stefan responds in the affirmative but then adds, "I also love my wife." Anne insists that this is impossible: "And you also love Gabriele, you also love Kirke, and maybe me too?" Katharina admonishes them to stop ruining the evening with this kind of talk—after all, she routinely frames her relationship with Stefan as one she has freely chosen—but a subsequent shot portrays her looking out the window contemplatively; poetic images of rain, trees, and puddles, one of which reflects the inverted figure of a church tower, underscore her melancholy mood.

A cut to the internal space of Stefan's apartment offers a stark juxtaposition to this melancholic atmosphere. Bright light and warm colors characterize this tableau at the family breakfast table, where Stefan jokes with his older son over bowls of cereal. Throughout the film, we almost never hear Magdalena speak, and the only words she utters here consist of an admonishment to her younger son to behave himself at the table. After breakfast, we see the family on a Sunday stroll by the river, where the twitter of birds fills the soundtrack as the children chase after squirrels. Later, back in the apartment, Stefan lies with his head on Magdalena's lap. She looks directly into the camera, her face framed in a close-up that simultaneously awakens curiosity about this quiet woman and reminds us that the rather idyllic family scenes we have just witnessed belie the fact of Stefan's extramarital affair. A final shot portrays Magdalena and Stefan sitting back-to-back on a child's cot; Stefan, holding a toy car, appears childlike, one more boy Magdalena must care for.

The disjunctive quality of these opening scenes, referred to by Turanskyj as its "cut-up" aesthetic, introduces the nonlinear narrative style of *Nine Lives*. The film's collage-like form was significantly influenced by Stöckl's education at the Ulm Film School, where *Nine Lives* was produced as her graduation film. A pedagogical innovation of film education at Ulm was the production of so-called miniatures, very short films that presented coherent dramaturgical units in and of themselves and could also be stitched together into longer works. The creation of miniatures presented a solution to the budgetary constraints of independent filmmaking, while also demanding of students close attention to the economy of form. As Stöckl later explained, "Thinking in miniatures enables you, even if you don't have money for a full feature film—which might consist of 25 or 30 miniatures—just to begin and to build onto that beginning later. For me, miniatures represent the principle of hope."[13] The concept of miniatures underpins the narrative form of *Nine Lives*, which made a virtue of the low-budget context in which it was produced. But as film historian Daniela Sannwald observes, the significance of the miniature principle is more than just a creative response to economic limitations: "In Stöckl's film jumping between situations—the eschewal of linearity—corresponds to the life paths of the main protagonists, who falter, stumble, change course, and jump" (184). This patchwork quality of the film thus figures the ways that Anne and Katharina navigate the process of self-realization in tension with institutions and norms; it also calls attention to the construction of *Nine Lives* as a film. By literally showing the film's own seams, this cut-up style foregrounds the process of (women's) artistic production, a theme that is echoed in Gabriele's creation of the pop song "The Cat Has Nine Lives" and in the many other scenes throughout the film that show characters in the process of making things: fashioning paper flowers, sketching with pencil, writing a newspaper article, test-launching a newly engineered airplane.

The Cat Has Nine Lives presents a chain of set pieces, with dream images, flashbacks, and music videos interspersed with the more conventional dramatic scenes through which the film's storyline unfolds, a narrative form that the miniature principle helps to explain. The idea of the miniature is also crucial to the feminist aesthetics that Stöckl develops, since it aids in the process of unsettling clear demarcations between fantasy and reality and between documentary, autofiction, and narrative feature, disrupting the conventions of genre and spectatorship. This disruption is further achieved through editing and cinematography. Like other new-wave films, *Nine Lives* breaks with the style of continuity editing, rarely following the expected pattern of shot/reverse-shot and instead liberally employing jump cuts and smash cuts along with an occasional violation of the 180-degree rule. Along with these editing choices, rapid pans and extended long takes foreground the operations of the cinematic apparatus. At the same time, haptic strategies interrupt the preeminence of vision by appealing to senses that exceed film's technological capacities of representation, including touch, taste, and smell. These strategies aid the project of fostering self-reflection about (women's) representation in and viewership of dominant cinema; they are also key to the pleasurable experience of watching *Nine Lives*.

The most noteworthy generator of viewing pleasure in Stöckl's film, however, is its remarkable use of color, which relied on a complicated Technicolor grading process unusual in low-budget films of the era to capture the vibrant palette of the urban vistas, nature scenes, and 1960s-era fashion depicted in the film. In this regard, *Nine Lives* exemplifies what feminist film theorist Claire Johnston would later describe as women's counter-cinema. Decrying the "non-interventionist" style of women's filmmaking inspired by cinema verité, Johnston proclaimed, "Any revolutionary strategy must challenge the depiction of reality; it is not enough to discuss the oppression of women within the text of the film; the language of the cinema/the depiction of reality must also be interrogated, so that a break between ideology and text is effected."[14] Johnston called on women filmmakers to embrace the pleasurable tools of "illusionistic narrative film": "In order to counter our objectification in the cinema, our collective fantasies must be released: women's cinema must embody the working through of desire: such an objective demands the use of entertainment film" (31). The lush color, mythical characters, fantastical sequences, and collage aesthetics of *Nine Lives* all work to intervene in and thereby interrogate conventional depictions of reality and cinematic form in Johnston's sense, opening up new pathways for portraying women on screen and new forms of imagining resistance.

1968 and German History

The Cat Has Nine Lives premiered in the epochal year 1968. Throughout Europe and much of the world, that year signaled a caesura, as the student movement's revolt against the Vietnam War and its broader opposition to the status quo of capitalism, the political establishment, and traditional culture initiated significant social change. In addition to the confrontation with legacies of colonialism and imperialism that shaped this era, 1968 marked a particular reckoning with the Nazi past in West Germany, as a new generation of young people born during and after World War II confronted their elders about their wartime activities and their participation in or complicity with the crimes of the Holocaust.

The specific trajectory of German history was implicated not only in the personal and intergenerational confrontation with the Nazi past but also in the public and political events of "the long 1968" in the Federal Republic. Divided Germany's geopolitical position as ground zero of the Cold War led to the emergence, already in the 1950s, of a broad-based peace movement that paved the way for later antiwar activism by protesting—with support from the powerful trade unions—against both German rearmament and the proliferation of nuclear weapons. Drawing on the momentum of this movement, the SDS became a major voice in West German politics in the 1960s, taking the leading role in the Extraparliamentary Opposition (Außerparlamentarische Opposition, APO) against the government's plan to pass a series of emergency laws. Because they resonated with a similar set of laws that had facilitated Hitler's rise to power in the 1930s, the emergency laws became a flashpoint for public resistance against the authoritarianism of the West German government and its institutions, strengthening support for the APO and the New Left, which called attention to the many former Nazis still occupying positions of authority in the Federal Republic of Germany (FRG). Public support of the APO was buttressed in the wake of the shocking events of June 2, 1967, when the police shot and killed the twenty-six-year-old student Benno Ohnesorg during a demonstration against the Shah of Iran, who was visiting West Berlin. Ohnesorg's murder transformed the APO into a full-fledged student-led revolt.

On September 13, 1968, at the twenty-third delegate conference of the SDS in Frankfurt am Main, Helke Sander gave a speech in which she outlined both the theoretical basis of women's oppression and the practical work of the Action Council for the Liberation of Women to combat it. Although the speech indicted the SDS for reproducing patriarchal structures in both its organization and its political platform, Sander emphasized that the Action Council hoped to ally itself with the SDS and called on its male leaders to discuss the women's demands, concluding that, if they were not prepared to address the issue of women's emancipation, "then we must conclude that the SDS is nothing more than a puffed-up, counterrevolutionary yeast dough."[15] As it happened, the leadership did refuse any discussion of Sander's theses and instead insisted on moving forward with the meeting's prepared agenda. In response, activist Sigrid Rüger, who was visibly pregnant, pelted the men with tomatoes, an event that went down in history as the *Tomatenwurf* ("tomato toss") that started the West German women's movement. Not only the events surrounding the speech but also the theoretical framework Sander began to articulate in it paved the way for the development of feminist activism and thought in subsequent years:

> the division between private life and social life permanently relegates women to bearing the conflict of their own isolation individually. they continue to be socialized for private life and for the family, which in turn is dependent on conditions of production that we combat. this socialization into a particular role, the feelings of inferiority that derive from it, and the contradiction between their own expectations and the demands of society, lead to women's persistent guilty conscience about not being able to live up to the burdens placed on them, or to a sense of having to choose between alternatives, which in every case would entail the renunciation of vital needs and desires. (58, orthography in the original)

As Sander explained, women could not solve their social oppression on an individual basis, nor could they wait for the revolution, which—as demonstrated by the socialist countries—would not necessarily resolve the contradictions associated with private life. Thus, Sander called for collective action on behalf of women's emancipation now, and she went on to focus in particular on the Action Council's efforts to establish *Kinderläden*, alternative childcare organizations that served the twin purposes of alleviating the double burden faced by women with children and developing antiauthoritarian educational structures with the aim of socializing the next generation differently.

Despite the SDS's refusal to take up the issue of women's emancipation, the Action Council's emphasis on transforming early childhood education resonated with the broader focus of the student movement on pursuing a "long march through the institutions." Coined by SDS leader Rudi Dutschke, this motto described the activist strategy of laying the groundwork for revolution by transforming the establishment, both through the subversion of existing institutions including the university, the professions, and the media, and by fostering counterinstitutions. Although the SDS eventually dissolved in 1970 following protracted internal debates that splintered the organization, the long march through the institutions continued, leading to diverse developments including the founding of the Green Party, university reform, and the flourishing of alternative media, developments that contributed to the transformation of postwar German politics and society. Offering a nascent archive of the long 1968, *Nine Lives* makes these developments visible at the moment of their emergence.

"Power-War-Love"

Ula Stöckl was born in Ulm in 1938, and her life was deeply affected by World War II. Like many of her contemporaries in the student movement, she was too young to fully comprehend what was transpiring around her in the early 1940s, but the quest to understand the Nazi past and work through wartime trauma profoundly shaped her subsequent pursuits, including her filmmaking. Stöckl's father, a musician in the orchestra of the Ulm city theater, served at the front beginning in 1941. During the war, Ulm was heavily damaged by bombings, and in 1944, Stöckl's childhood home was destroyed, leaving her family destitute. Between 1943 and 1946, Stöckl's three younger siblings all died, one from a grenade strike and two owing to lack of access to medical care when they became gravely ill. A follower of the Nazi cause, Stöckl's father survived the war, but he struggled to find gainful employment again after receiving a two-year *Berufsverbot* (employment ban) as part of denazification proceedings. As a result, the family continued to live in precarious circumstances well into the postwar period, with Stöckl's mother—an uneducated woman who grew up in an orphanage run by nuns—taking on physically demanding menial jobs to put food on the table. As Stöckl later wrote, "These wartime and postwar memories and experiences . . . left a deep impression on my life. In hindsight, they explain the themes I chose, which reappear in all of my films. Again and again, there is a focus on father figures and the role of mothers, on generations, sex and relationship questions, family structures, work and love."[16] These themes come together in what Stöckl describes as her filmmaking motto, "Power-War-Love," a triumvirate that captures her exploration of patriarchal structures and gender roles, the role of violence and authoritarianism in upholding them, as well as the possibility of opposing them through love: "From stories I have learned that love is the most vital force, even when bombs are raining down and adversity prevails" (104). Indeed, Stöckl's films exhibit a utopian strain, a hopefulness regarding the possibility of shaping a different future, in particular through women's pursuit of subjectivity, sovereignty, and agency, not least in matters of sexuality and love. This hopefulness about the future resonates with the antiauthoritarian rallying cry of the 1968 student movement, "Phantasie an die Macht!" (All Power to the Imagination!), a catchphrase that *Nine Lives* transposes into cinematic form.

Stöckl's confrontation with power and war accelerated when, at the age of twenty, she traveled to Paris to work as an au pair. Arriving in 1958, she experienced firsthand the political turmoil surrounding the Algerian War of Independence, including a failed coup d'état in Algiers against newly installed Prime Minister Pierre Pflimlin, whose advocacy for negotiations with Algerian nationalists fighting for sovereignty led to violent uprisings by French settlers in Algeria, propelling Pflimlin's resignation after only twenty-one days in office. Shocked by these events and by the French treatment of Algerians more broadly, Stöckl challenged her French employers, who in turn accused her of hypocrisy, forcing her to begin reckoning with the Nazi past for the first time. In 1960, Stöckl moved to London, where she worked for a Jewish family who likewise engaged her in discussions about the Holocaust; it was in their home that she saw images of Auschwitz for the first time. The fact that Stöckl first learned about the details of the Nazi genocide of the Jews while living in Paris and London was indicative of the widespread silence, even amnesia, about the recent past that typified the 1950s in West Germany, and which the student movement of the 1960s sought to redress.

Stöckl has said that she lacked the vocabulary and the educational background to participate in the political activism associated with 1968 but that she charted a connection to its project through her artistic work.[17] Likewise, the language of feminism was not yet available to her when she wrote and directed *Nine Lives*, even as the film itself anticipates concerns that would shape the women's movement and subsequent feminist filmmaking. As Stöckl recalled in 2014, "A self-critical perspective about gender relations began to emerge for me—indeed, the idea practically suggested itself to people of my generation. To analyze violence, power, and domination/totalitarianism became my feminist life's work, which came together in the rallying cry 'The personal is political.'"[18] Stöckl's earliest films, including *Nine Lives*, are dedicated to elucidating the connections between personal experience and political structures summed up in this phrase.

In 1954, before moving abroad, Stöckl had completed secretarial training, pursuing one of the main professional pathways open to women in the 1950s. After gaining competency in French and English while employed as an au pair, she returned to Paris to work as an executive secretary in the early 1960s. Although this position brought her a measure of financial independence and social mobility, Stöckl was bored by the work. The tension she experienced, between the desire for security and the need for self-expression and critical engagement with the world, is explicitly addressed through the character of Katharina in *Nine Lives*.

An abrupt cut from the apartment of Stefan and Magdalena places us in an office, where Katharina, wearing her glasses, sits at a desk negotiating a salary. In a long take, the camera holds on her image in the center of the screen before cutting to an even closer shot of her face. Although we hear the voice of the man she is negotiating with, we don't see him at first; instead, we register the effects of his words on Katharina, who remains the focus of this scene. She is applying for a job as an executive secretary, a position for which she is clearly well qualified, but the employer wonders why Katharina would want to leave behind her work as a freelance journalist, which must be very interesting and allow her a less regimented existence than nine-to-five office work. Reflecting her own internal conflict, Katharina is uncomfortable answering the question and finally replies, "Let's assume I'm currently making little progress [as a freelancer.]" Later, Katharina explains that she had no real intention of returning to secretarial work but wanted to see if she could still secure a regular job, since knowing she had a fallback position—and that she could obtain a good salary—would be self-affirming.

For Ula Stöckl, the path to becoming a filmmaker likewise entailed stepping away from the security of secretarial work and into the unknown. While working in Paris, Stöckl began to write stories. After returning to Germany she took up a secretarial position in Stuttgart and later worked as an editorial assistant in the television department of a music production firm, where she became interested in writing screenplays. When she failed to find opportunities for advancement at the firm, however, Stöckl realized that her lack of professional training was holding her back. She inquired at the newly established Ulm Film School about the possibility of studying screenwriting there and learned that the school's courses entailed a holistic approach to training aspiring filmmakers: rather than taking discrete courses in screenwriting, directing, or producing, students would learn all dimensions of the process. Lacking any visible role models, Stöckl had not even considered the possibility of directing and shooting films herself, but she was encouraged to apply. When she enrolled at the Ulm Film School in 1962, Ula Stöckl became the very first woman film student in West Germany.

Creating the New German Feature Film

The reshaping of education and the media constituted focal points for the New Left in West Germany, where the ongoing process of dismantling authoritarian institutions and democratizing the public sphere continued throughout the postwar period. Film history is closely intertwined with these developments. Already in 1962, when twenty-six young filmmakers gathered at the Oberhausen Short Film Festival to declare their intention "to create the new German feature film," these signatories of the Oberhausen Manifesto had three goals in mind: the establishment of a foundation that would enable young filmmakers to create their first feature films; subsidies to support independent short films as venues for experimentation; and "the creation of an intellectual center for film, in which new generations can be trained and in which theoretical work and developmental work have their place."[19] In short order, the Oberhausen group made headway on achieving all three of these goals by garnering institutional and financial support for film training and alternative filmmaking practices, support that transformed the enterprise of cinema in West Germany in the following years.

The ambition of creating an intellectual center for film in the FRG came to fruition first, when signatories Alexander Kluge, Edgar Reitz, and Detten Schleiermacher cofounded the film department at the Hochschule für Gestaltung in Ulm (HfG; Ulm School of Design). Writing in 1962, Kluge described the department: "This institution has been established as of October 1, and it consists of twelve instructors, i.e., two film scholars and ten directors, and to all appearances it is off to a good start. This Department for Film Design in connection with the Scholl-Siblings Foundation (in keeping with the *Bauhaus* conception) links new filmic models with instruction in film design."[20] Kluge alludes here to the history of the HfG, which was founded in 1953 by Inge Scholl, Otl Aicher, and Max Bill as the postwar successor institution to the Bauhaus, the influential school of art and design founded by Walter Gropius in Weimar in 1919 and later shut down by the Nazis (Scholl was the sister of Hans and Sophie Scholl, who were executed for their roles in the White Rose student resistance movement against the Third Reich). The HfG had offered film instruction for several years, but after the Oberhausen Manifesto it formalized film as a course of study, offering training grounded on the principle of combining education in film theory, research, and praxis.

The creation of the Ulm film department was followed by the founding of several other institutions that furthered the Oberhauseners' goals of developing an intellectual foundation for filmmaking in West Germany. These included a centralized film archive, the Stiftung Deutsche Kinemathek (German Cinematheque Foundation, 1963) and two further film schools, the Deutsche Film- und Fernsehakademie Berlin (dffb; German Film and Television Academy, 1966) and the Hochschule für Film und Fernsehen in Munich (HFF; School of Film and Television, 1967). Formalized in 1967, the Kuratorium Junger Deutscher Film (Committee for Young German Film) was explicitly tasked with putting the manifesto's financial proposals into practice: with government funding administered by a board of film journalists, the Kuratorium financed twenty feature films between 1965 and 1968, including the first features of Kluge, *Yesterday Girl* (*Abschied von gestern*, 1966), and Reitz, *Lust for Love* (*Mahlzeiten*, 1967), as well as Stöckl's *The Cat Has Nine Lives*.

There were no women among the twenty-six filmmakers who signed the Oberhausen Manifesto in 1962. As film scholar Claudia Lenssen explains, "At the time, the right to artistic self-realization in film had obvious masculine connotations, and the cultural power to control its interpretation was solidly anchored in patriarchal rituals."[21] Many groundbreaking films of the New German Cinema (NGC) did, however, feature women protagonists, who appeared as seismographs of social and political change in the 1960s. Like their counterparts in French, Italian, and Swedish new-wave films, these women characters represented a new kind of screen femininity that broke with the stereotypical paradigms for representing women that had predominated in the "Papa's Cinema" of the 1950s—ingenues, bombshells, and melodramatic mothers. Instead, women characters in new-wave films often indexed the search for individual experience in a repressive society, exhibiting spontaneity, immediacy, and unruliness. Yet, as many commentators have noted, insofar as they functioned as allegories of postwar social and political conditions, women in new-wave films often remained bound by the constraints of heteropatriarchy—indeed, it was precisely their reproductive capacity that was harnessed for representative purposes in these films.[22]

The first features of Kluge and Reitz, which were shot during their tenure at the Ulm HfG, were no exception. Kluge's *Yesterday Girl* follows the itinerant Anita G., played by the director's sister, Alexandra Kluge. A refugee from East Germany, this symbolic character is the daughter of Jewish Holocaust survivors, former factory owners whose property has been expropriated. A figure for the unassimilated burdens of German history, Anita drifts through Frankfurt am Main carrying a suitcase, trying her hand at odd jobs, seeking in vain to enroll at the university, and pursuing an affair with the married government official Pichota (Günter Mack), who breaks off the relationship after Anita becomes pregnant. Hounded by the law for a series of minor infractions—at the outset of the film she stands trial for stealing a colleague's cardigan sweater, and later she runs out on a hotel bill—Anita eventually turns herself in to the police and lands in a women's prison, where she gives birth to a child who is taken away by the state.

Reitz's *Lust for Love* follows protagonist Elisabeth (Heidi Stroh), who gives up on studying photography when she marries the medical student Rolf (Georg Hauke) and gives birth to five children in short order. Elisabeth's fertility indexes her voracious appetite for bodily pleasures: parties, games, sex, and the "mealtimes" of the film's German title. Increasingly alienated by the vitality and lustiness that initially attracted him to Elisabeth, Rolf finds himself unable to withstand the financial and psychological pressures of family life. After quitting medical school, he fails to make it as a pharmaceutical salesman, and he increasingly withdraws from his wife and children. In search of social connections, Elisabeth opens up to the Mormon missionaries who appear at her door, and she and Rolf eventually convert to Mormonism in a riverside baptismal ceremony. The conversion does not, however, represent a redemption for Rolf, whose desperation leads to his death by suicide. In the film's rather dystopian ending, Elisabeth takes the only path that seemingly remains open to her as a young widow with five children: she embraces the instrumentalization of her body as a birthing machine, marries a Mormon elder, and immigrates with her children to America.

In both Kluge's and Reitz's films, mother figures are imbued with allegorical significance: "they are symbolically charged with carrying the burden of the future, while having, at the same time, no place to go."[23] In this regard, as John Urang has written about *Yesterday Girl*, "procreation functions less as a marker of the specificity of women's experience than as a cipher for more general questions of social renewal."[24] *Yesterday Girl* and *Lust for Love* both engage with women's biological reproduction in order to think through problems of cultural reproduction and creation (of art, of film, of social institutions) in the aftermath of World War II and Nazism, and in the context of ongoing struggles over the public sphere in the postwar Federal Republic.

Conceived of and realized during the period when Stöckl was studying there, both films involved extensive collaboration by members of the Ulm film department. *Yesterday Girl* was shot by Edgar Reitz and cinematographer Thomas Mauch, who served for a time on the faculty of the HfG; Mauch also shot *Lust for Love*, on which Kluge served as a script consultant. Ula Stöckl worked on both *Yesterday Girl* and *Lust for Love*, serving in an official capacity as the assistant director for Reitz's film; later, she would go on to collaborate with Reitz on the experimental assemblage film *Stories of the Dumpster Kid* (*Geschichten vom Kübelkind*, 1971). Forged in the creative context of this period at Ulm, *Nine Lives* involved many of the same collaborators who worked on Kluge's and Reitz's films, perhaps most notably the cinematographer Mauch (whose work on the film is uncredited but well documented) and the actress Stroh, who plays the pop singer Gabriele. In addition to sharing personnel, the artistic vision of Stöckl's film was significantly influenced by her mentors, even as *Nine Lives* breaks in important ways with the gendered forms of representation that characterize their work.

In searching for paradigmatic women characters, Stöckl regularly drew throughout her filmmaking career on the allegorical qualities of classical mythological figures, including Antigone (the subject of her first short film *Antigone*, 1964), Circe in *Nine Lives*, and Medea in *The Sleep of Reason* (*Der Schlaf der Vernunft*, 1984). In depicting these characters, however, Stöckl interprets them anew, seeking to liberate them from the patriarchal contexts out of which they emerged. Likewise, women characters in *Nine Lives* do not function as seismographs of the postwar condition, and the barriers posed by marriage, biological reproduction, and motherhood do not serve as metaphors in the film. Rather, the main protagonists of *Nine Lives* refuse socially prescribed roles for women, striving to emancipate themselves sexually (Magdalena is the exception that proves the rule, serving as a reminder of the pitfalls of marriage and domestic life for women, and she notably remains a minor character). This utopian strain of Stöckl's film—imagining alternatives rather than picturing the inexorable process of women's entrapment and downfall—is a key component of the nascent feminist vision of *Nine Lives*.

An early sequence featuring a cameo appearance by Edgar Reitz condenses the film's critique of the patriarchal sexual imagination and its imbrication with dominant cinematic language. At an outdoor café, Katharina sits with a man played by Reitz in a covered swing, a piece of furniture notably referred to in German as a "Hollywood-Schaukel" (Hollywood swing). Anne arrives at the café and climbs onto Katharina's lap, another moment of close physical intimacy shared by the two women. Voyeuristically observing them, Reitz expresses his inability to concentrate on the conversation anymore when he sees the women embracing; as he suggests, "We could recover the natural order of things if I took your place." After they follow his suggestion to switch places, Reitz wryly notes, "Our eroticism is simply patriarchal. It can't be helped I'm afraid" (fig. 5). Here, Reitz—the film professor and rising star of the indubitably masculinist NGC—rather satirically serves as the mouthpiece for the sociocultural and aesthetic problem posed by *Nine Lives*: what Stöckl later described as the attempt to break free from the male gaze in order to find metaphors for women's desire.[25] Moreover,

Our eroticism is simply patriarchal.

Figure 5. Attempting to break free of the male gaze: Edgar Reitz's cameo appearance on the "Hollywood swing."

as film scholar Sabine Schöbel describes it, "On the meta-level of the 'Hollywood swing,' the scene and the director who appears in it represent a narrative tradition that is grounded in the separation of its female characters"—most often by pitting them against one another in a love triangle—a tradition that Stöckl's film refutes by insistently uniting and reuniting Anne and Katharina.[26]

Although it was short-lived—the film department dissolved when the HfG, in a reprise of the fate of the Bauhaus, was shut down by the government for political reasons in 1968—the Ulm School played a significant role in the development of a new film culture in West Germany, paving the way for the emergence of both the NGC and the feminist film movement. Indeed, a noteworthy aspect of the Ulm film department was its inclusion of women, who were well represented among the students enrolled there.[27] Stöckl's fellow classmates Jeanine Meerapfel (who joined the department in 1963), Claudia von Alemann (who joined in 1964), and Recha Jungmann (also 1964) all went on to make important feature and documentary films in the 1970s and 1980s.[28]

The writings of the Frankfurt School provided a significant theoretical anchoring for film education at the HfG: "Like literature and science, film should constitute a form of knowledge and imagination that orients itself to reality as a whole."[29] Yet, as Kluge wrote in the 1964 essay "Die Utopie Film," in which he outlined the pedagogical principles undergirding his conception of film education, "Film and television, in contrast to the classical arts and literature, possess a mass basis. They rely on reproduced reality and they represent interventions into that reality. Precisely because film appears as reality, these interventions always already involve an alteration of that reality, and for this reason they entail a special responsibility."[30] This responsibility must be cultivated so that the individual filmmaker is in possession of a conscience "in intellectual, artistic, economic, and political regards," and it is for this reason that "film education cannot be technical training alone" (1140).

In turn, a capacious film education can help unfold the promise of cinema: "Precisely because one can (with the help of the apparatus) do everything with film, one can also tell the truth with it: no other medium can record thoughts in the same way as film does; the perspectives of the camera are not limited to normal human perspectives" (1144–45). Film pedagogy at Ulm was oriented toward the development of new cinematic forms to realize this potential, not least the miniature, which became an animating principle in the work of both the HfG's students and its instructors. Much of Kluge's prolific filmmaking over six decades has been informed by the concept of the miniature, a form that he particularly embraces in his work for television and in his *Minutenfilme*, short films of one to eight minutes that distill complex ideas from cultural history by employing a distinctive mode of editing that facilitates remarkable assemblages of sound and image.

In a companion piece to Kluge's essay titled "Utopie Kino," written between 1963 and 1965, Edgar Reitz likewise described the conception of cinema that informed his teaching in Ulm and his own early filmmaking. Reitz conceptualizes a new "analytical film" that stands in contrast to the three foundational genres of conventional cinema, the feature, the documentary, and the experimental film. The analytical film is not bound by a formal style but rather aims to dismantle conventional categories and methods of filmmaking, adopting a range of techniques to facilitate its analysis of reality: "deconstruction, transformation, making unrecognizable, making visible, making aware, gaining and creating freedom vis-à-vis the object, making available."[31] As Reitz explains, "According to Adorno, until now most films are nothing more than 'propaganda for the world as it exists,' a world that is not subject to transformation. [The analytical film] deconstructs the existing world into its various elements; once these have been liberated from the constraining circumstances and stereotypes associated with them, the imagination can begin to engage with them again" (18).

Accordingly, hands-on education at the HfG cultivated competency in the use of cameras, lighting, and editing, as well as producing, and students were encouraged to develop their own aesthetic approaches to unmasking reality through film. Although Ula Stöckl had entered the school with a primary interest in studying screenwriting, the model of education pursued by Kluge and Reitz prepared students to become film authors: to take over and understand every aspect of the filmmaking process. As Stöckl recalled in 2012, "Figuring out and following through on my own interests was the most important thing for me at first, especially as a woman. Being able to do everything myself when necessary has remained an essential proposition for me. 'If you have done everything yourself, then you can also explain it and you know that it works!,' Edgar Reitz would say, 'Then no one can tell you differently!'"[32] Yet, as Stöckl went on to note, "With this doctrine I quickly ran up against gender-specific boundaries—the first cameraman I encountered didn't want a woman touching the technology" (110). In a 1977 interview, Stöckl elaborated on the process of gaining the confidence to articulate her authorial vision as a filmmaker and also to achieve it on set: "What I have now learned after all these years, what I have begun to specialize in more and more, is to listen only and exclusively to myself at these times, to become as egotistical as I possibly can, since everything else has only caused me harm."[33] Giving up on being likable, and reconciling herself to the loneliness of the directorial experience, were precursors, in Stöckl's account, to her ability to realize her vision as a woman filmmaker.

Language

The difficulty of women's self-expression, especially in exchange with insensitive and patronizing men, is made palpable again and again in *Nine Lives*. Like the scene with Edgar Reitz that precedes it, a lengthy set piece portraying a conversation between Anne and Sascha (Alexander Kaempfe), a friend and potential love interest, offers an ironic take on this theme by charting Anne's attempt to assert herself in the face of a consummate mansplainer's arrogant discourse. An analytical scene in Reitz's sense, this miniature makes visible and deconstructs for the viewer the problem of gendered communication, revealing Anne's frustration at Sascha's refusal to listen, his dictation of normative modes of conduct, and his male fragility when she tries to talk back. Exemplary of the constant interchange between French and German that characterizes the film more broadly, the code-switching in this sequence highlights the gendering of linguistic conventions and the performativity of gender roles, while also drawing attention to the intersections of sexual and gender identity with national identity. A competent French speaker, Sascha repeatedly draws Anne in by addressing her in her native language: in French he speaks with her rather cautiously and politely. But as soon as he falters or senses that Anne is gaining the upper hand, Sascha immediately switches to German, a move that facilitates his mastery of the conversation by allowing him to push his claims in his mother tongue and to discombobulate Anne by forcing her to shift between registers.

The dialog begins when Anne, speaking in French, asks: "Why was it, the other day, that you told me I should be good? What does that mean?" Sascha replies, "Good means good," and then, switching to German, he elaborates on his view that being good means articulating what one wants and consistently acting on it. "Oui, d'accord," Anne responds, "but being consistent requires certainty." "Of course, but [one] can make choosing easier by being consistent beforehand," Sascha replies, suggesting that individual behavior should follow from a predetermined code of ethics. While they speak, the camera remains largely static, framing Anne and Sascha in a full shot, but a series of jump cuts disrupts the continuity of the sequence, calling our attention both to the eternal recurrence of conversations like this one and to the cinematic construction of the scene. The jump cuts operate as a defamiliarization effect, in the

Brechtian sense, to unmask the artifice of both patriarchal discourse and the cinematic apparatus.

While both speakers have used the impersonal "one" [*man*] throughout, Anne now switches to the second person, addressing Sascha directly: "So you can't do any old thing, and thus nor can I?" When Sascha affirms this dictum, Anne pushes back.

> Anne: "Yes I can. *I always do what I want.*"
> Sascha [*in French*]: "Not with me."
> Anne: "So I'll do nothing with you."
> Sascha [*in French*]: "And not with my friends."
> Anne: "Just because I'm here with you today and smile at you and give you a flower, must I do this every day for you?"
> Sascha [*laughing*]: "Of course."
> Anne: "You're [crazy]."

Anne and Sascha continue to spar with each other, constantly switching between French and German. Again and again, Sascha insists that normative standards of conduct must be upheld, eventually revealing a certain self-consciousness about his reliance on others (women) to prop up his psyche: "I expect a person to keep to the style of that very person, as initially and voluntarily presented to me. Freely. . . . I have a certain, a certain soul, let us say, with a given function of feeling and certain adherences as determined during childhood which should remain inviolate." Anne, however, persists in demanding the possibility of spontaneity: "I don't want to stop. Why should I? Nothing is ever definitive. Today is today, tomorrow, tomorrow."

As Sascha continues to insist that Anne is personally responsible for the well-being of those around her, an abrupt cut shows the two characters in medium shot, and Anne responds: "You've no right to call me a capitalist for offering you my sympathy but nothing more. It's disgusting" (fig. 6). Sascha says, "Capitalism is. . . . It is not

You've no right to call me a capitalist

Figure 6. The dialog between Anne and Sascha (Alexander Kaempfe) indexes everyday sexism.

only politics." We now see the couple from yet another new angle, as Anne inquires, "Because your vanity is wounded, do you think I'm not searching?" "That's not searching," Sascha replies, "Going round in circles is not searching. It's a circle that you're in." Echoing this dialog, the camera reverses angles here to capture Anne and Sascha from behind, in a medium close-up that frames them tightly between two trees, their faces obscured, emphasizing the stifling circularity of their conversation. Framed in this way, Anne speaks again, uttering one of the key lines of the film, which aligns the patriarchal oppression of women with fascist control:

> Anne: "So you reject that I might live in this atmosphere? You won't admit that I can only live in a certain atmosphere because it's not yours. That's fascism. You reject my approach. Why?"
> Sascha: "Because it's not viable in the long-term."
> Anne: "But that's my problem. It's not viable for you, but it is for me. Ridiculous!"
> Sascha: "It's not for most people."
> Anne: "I'm not most people. I am me! So . . . it's my problem. I can't live differently to how I do."
> Sascha: "At least try not to hurt your. . . ."

In the concluding dialog of this lengthy scene, Anne finally pinpoints the male fragility at the heart of Sascha's attempt to assert control over her behavior and lifestyle: "I didn't hurt you more than you did me, Sascha. I'd like to get this straight. Don't believe it's others that hurt you. You might think [about how] you hurt people, too. You're not the only one. . . ." Sascha responds, "But why do we hurt people?" Anne gets the final word, however: "I don't know. You tell me, smart ass. You're so rational and advanced. Explain it to me!"

By indexing—as here—with great detail and precision the (at times rather banal) conversations through which everyday sexism is asserted and naturalized, *Nine Lives* offers an analytic view of the way structures of power and domination are reproduced within personal relationships. As the dialog between Anne and Sascha also directly suggests, the quest to transform these structures was a significant pursuit of the 1968 student revolt—and then of the women's movement—not least because emancipatory relations between the sexes constituted a key site for breaking with the fascism that had imprinted the family dynamics, domestic lives, and intimate affairs of the parents' generation. This scene, however, also demonstrates the laborious process of attempting such an emancipation. As Anne articulates the necessity of breaking out of prescribed roles in order to assert her own subjectivity, Sascha repeatedly reels her back in, insisting that her quest for alternatives is illegitimate and her lifestyle is both unethical and unsustainable. The camera's claustrophobic framing of the two characters emphasizes the suffocating quality of their interaction, and Sascha's unsympathetic nature is underscored by the casting choice of the nonprofessional actor who plays him, Alexander Kaempfe, a prominent translator of Russian literature who was notorious in the bohemian circles of 1960s-era Munich for his relentless pursuit of younger women. Just as jump cuts repeatedly interrupt this sequence, fracturing our perception of time and the illusion of cinematic continuity, Anne and Sascha's constant switching between French and German likewise calls attention to the instability and the constraining force of language itself.

Stöckl has described her choice to cast a nonnative speaker of German, her friend Kristine de Loup, as one of the protagonists in her film as a deliberate one that allowed her to introduce the theme of multilingualism into *Nine Lives*: "This was also part of my idea of realism, since we all engage with people every day who are not perfect speakers of our language."[34] Anne's questions about standard German formulations and phrases, occasional mispronunciations and malapropisms, as well as her code-switching, all serve to denaturalize the transparency of linguistic signification as such. As when Stefan assertively tries to teach Anne to pronounce the consonant "H" or when Sascha repeatedly insists that their conversation be carried out in German rather than French, linguistic difference helps call attention to gendered modes of communication. As Stöckl further explains, "From an early age I harbored great doubts about language, in the sense that I really couldn't say to what extent language is able to convey what I really want to express. How does what I'm talking about actually come across?" (118). This skepticism about the communicative potential of language underpins Stöckl's interest in depicting how conversations across languages can both disrupt and supplement the creation of meaning.

Multilingual dialog and the casting of non-German actors represent a facet of Stöckl's authorial vision that is also on view in her later films, especially the 1984 film *The Sleep of Reason*, for which the Italian actor Ida Di Benedetto, who knew no German at all, learned the entire dialog phonetically for her role as the lead character Dr. Dea Janssen. Di Benedetto's brilliant performance as Dea draws on her denaturalized relation to the German lines she speaks to capture the dis-ease with patriarchal discourse that her character, based on Medea, epitomizes. Not least through this performative disruption of monolingualism, the character of Dea figures the transnational dimensions of women's oppression while also calling attention to the specific ways in which this oppression is sedimented in German culture, extending the critique articulated in the dialog between Anne and Sascha in *Nine Lives*.

Colors

Anne wears a bright red dress, and Sascha is clothed in a Loden green sweater; the sharp contrast of their costumes' complementary colors is set off against the hues of the pastoral scene in which their dialog unfolds: the light green grass of the forest floor and the gray-brown bark of the trees. Here and throughout Stöckl's film, the vibrant color palette—awash in reds, greens, and yellows—accentuates differences between characters while also contributing significantly to the visual pleasures of the film. *The Cat Has Nine Lives* relied on a time-consuming color grading process to achieve the luminous tones that give vivid expression to the multihued flowers and plants, candy-colored dresses, and psychedelic fantasy sequences that predominate in its kaleidoscopic mise-en-scène. This use of color—along with the widescreen format in which it was shot—is crucial to the film's vitality and to the tactile, haptic forms of spectatorship it promotes; its glowing color palette also aligns *Nine Lives* with the aesthetics of pop.

This pop aesthetic significantly contributed to the negative reception of *Nine Lives* as unserious and superficial upon its debut in 1968: its deliberate use of bright colors presents a sharp contrast to the black-and-white cinematography and muted color schemes that tended to predominate in both early NGC films and the feminist cinema of the 1970s. In fact, the format that Stöckl chose was typically employed by genre films of the period, not by new-wave films that sought to engage critically with cinematic form. Stöckl explained the choice to adopt this format in a 1969 interview:

> I actually see black and white as a form of defamiliariza-
> tion, while color for me—in contrast to the dominant

practice—seems much more documentary-like. I liked the Techniscope process because Westerns were shot that way, and I imagined that one could make a really great tearjerker, a Heimatfilm, in this format. It would really lend itself to that, because [the color process] packages the whole story in another dimension. And I found that essential for the theme of the film: it really unfolds in all the girls' kitschiest places, and these kitschy places mean color. Whether it becomes palpable for others or just for me, everything that people do in this film hurts. This is what I capture in the colors.[35]

Stöckl's explanation emphasizes her appropriation of the formal language of genre films—Westerns, melodramas, and the unique German genre of the Heimatfilm—harnessing their use of saturated colors to highlight the tensions between artifice and candor, surface presentation and interiority, in ways that anticipate strategies later employed by Rainer Werner Fassbinder in his resignification of Hollywood melodrama. Stöckl's statement points to a homology, but also a tension, between color and femininity specifically. As she suggests, color is necessary to convey the ostensible vulgarity and excess attached to the feminine, but also the pain that is produced by its regulation and policing, as in the dialog between Anne and Sascha discussed above. Color gives vibrant expression to the milieu of Munich in 1968 and the women's struggles to assert themselves, but by "packaging the whole story in a different dimension" it also distracts from the film's realism and endows this story with another level of meaning.

In his work on the fear of color in Western culture, the artist and critic David Batchelor explains that "Chromophobia manifests itself in the many and varied attempts to purge colour from culture, to devalue colour, to diminish its significance, to deny its complexity."[36] As Batchelor argues, this purging takes place via two interconnected operations: "In the first, colour is made out to be the property of some 'foreign' body—usually the feminine, the oriental, the primitive, the infantile, the vulgar, the queer or the pathological. In the second, colour is relegated to the realm of the superficial, the supplementary, the inessential or the cosmetic" (64). *Nine Lives* offers both a reflection on and a retort to this chromophobia with its assertive use of color and especially its alignment of women with flowers, candy, and other signifiers of the decorative and saccharine. Yet the film's reception was plagued by precisely the chromophobia that it seeks to critically unmask.

The first color film for both Stöckl and her cinematographers Dietrich Lohmann and Thomas Mauch, *Nine Lives* was filmed in Techniscope, a special system for shooting on 35mm developed by Technicolor Italy in 1960 that allowed the filmmakers to save celluloid (and therefore money) by creating twice as many images per frame as with the standard shooting format. Also referred to as 2-perf, the process involved the camera pulling down the negative by two perforations (rather than the standard four perforations), requiring half the amount of film stock for a film of the same running time; at 24 frames per second, Techniscope shoots 45 rather than 90 feet of film every minute. Although its aspect ratio is shallower than with standard shooting formats, 2-perf is easily cropped to widescreen. Since it is a production-only process, Techniscope films must be converted and enlarged for distribution, creating prints that can run on 4-perf projectors, a process that can lead to loss of image quality.

Stöckl, Lohmann, and Mauch used Kodak film and regular spherical lenses to shoot *Nine Lives*. Once the film had been edited, it was sent to Rome, where Techniscope Italy created a color-graded optical transfer print for exhibition.[37] The complicated color transfer process did not involve printing the Techniscope negative onto regular positive film. Rather, Technicolor process 5 was used to generate three color separations (cyan, magenta, and yellow), which were then printed by dye transfer onto blank film. Using a chemical process, the color separations were transferred onto relief matrices through which color was sequentially applied to the print. As explained by Claudia Gittel, who was involved in the color restoration of *Nine Lives* as part of the film's digitization, "[Technicolor process 5] functioned almost more like lithography than a traditional photochemical process. Because they were produced via a specialized—and highly complex—procedure, original Technicolor copies exhibit a unique, very intensive and saturated chromaticity, which is not comparable to a regular Eastman-Kodak color positive."[38]

Like other Techniscope films of the era—including Jean-Luc Godard's *Pierrot le Fou* (1965) and Sergio Leone's *Once upon a Time in the West* (1968)—*Nine Lives* makes a virtue out of this format, packing nearly every frame with abundant color and taking advantage of the graininess revealed by the transfer process to achieve the documentary-like verisimilitude that endows the film with immediacy and authenticity. Costuming comprises an especially crucial dimension of the film's mise-en-scène: while the male characters (especially Stefan) are routinely clothed entirely in black, and older, minor women characters often appear in beige and brown, the five central characters don multihued dresses and tops in a spectrum of colors including red, orange, and bright blue. For the most part, these clothes belonged to the actors themselves. The crew of *Nine Lives* did not include a costume or set designer; instead, the actors made their own costuming choices, wearing items that they had brought to the set and borrowing from Stöckl's own wardrobe, thereby amplifying the DIY and autobiographical dimensions of the film.[39]

Anne pulls on vibrant stalks of green grass before an abrupt cut places us inside the space of Sascha's apartment, where loud diegetic music signals that a party is underway. Katharina is dancing; snapping her fingers, she looks at Sascha, and we see his lips moving, but we can't hear what he says. Following directly on the lengthy dialog with Anne in the woods, this scene deprives Sascha of the power of speech through a play with diegetic sound, a wry comment on his abuse of that power earlier. Anne, wearing a different red dress, this one emblazoned with white flowers, dances with a tall hippie wearing an orange tunic, and a rapid montage shows us the dancing bodies and feet of the many revelers at this gathering. When the music ends, Anne withdraws from the group to sit on a low couch, where she finds a parcel of colored tissue paper. She unfurls a roll of red paper and then disappears into another room, where she begins to craft large, bright paper flowers. Suddenly, the party is filled with these decorative blooms. When another song begins to play, Anne and Sascha dance, and—following her established pattern—she asks him if he loves her, but then she tells Katharina that dancing with Sascha makes her sad and asks Katharina to step in. Anne lies in an intimate embrace with another man, the hippie she had been dancing with earlier, whom she also asks if he loves her; when he replies in the negative, she looks forlorn. Katharina comes into the room as Anne is sitting on the floor holding a large bouquet of paper flowers and asks how she is doing. Anne responds by vociferously declaring twice in a row how bored she is before presenting the bouquet to Katharina.[40]

A lovely two-shot shows the two women embracing, surrounded by colorful paper flowers, an image that summarizes the film's critical attention to the decorative role of women in patriarchal society and the difficulty of crafting alternative forms of representation (fig. 7). Accentuating this idea, Katharina tells Sascha that they are going to "plant" the artificial flowers in the English Garden, Munich's central park. We see the three figures in the pitch-black park, where Anne shouts, "Vive la liberté," and then sets her flowers ablaze, yelling, "I am Prometheus!" (fig. 8). By aligning herself with the Greek god credited with shaping humans from clay and helping them to establish civilization by granting them fire, Anne alludes to the elemental force of her own creativity but also to its thwarted and even tragic dimensions, as underscored by her immolation of the paper flowers she has spent the evening crafting.

Figure 7. Crafting alternative forms of representation to the decorative role of women: Anne and Katharina with paper flowers.

When the three characters return to the empty apartment, Sascha pours vodka and plays a recording of Russian folk music. Portrayed in a static long take that lasts for three full minutes, Sascha and Katharina dance in a close embrace as Anne awkwardly looks on. In a reprisal of the earlier scene in which she burned holes in her pantyhose, here Anne begins cutting this second skin again, turning into a destructive tool the scissors she had used previously to make the flowers. Sascha, who had at first courted Anne, tightly holds and then kisses Katharina, who accepts his advances. Although Anne had earlier rejected Sascha and demanded that Katharina take him off her hands, she now accuses Katharina of leading him on. Using the nickname she reserves for her friend when referring to her relations with men, Anne declares, "Stefanie, you're not fair! You're playing a game with Sascha." But when Katharina leads Sascha into the bedroom, Anne despondently remarks, "[I guess it wasn't a game after all!]" The camera slowly pans downward, holding on the empty room, a space that is dotted with the red and green colors that have dominated this sequence, before a cut to Anne's face reveals her crying tears of anger and frustration.

Anne's frustration results from the paradox that confronts her again and again in her relations with men throughout *Nine Lives*.

Figure 8. "I am Prometheus": Thwarted creativity on display.

On the one hand, she insists on her freedom, rejecting the demand for consistency placed upon her by her previous marriage and reiterated by Sascha as a male expectation of women in the dialog recounted above. On the other hand, this "freedom" is itself co-opted by the men Anne meets, like the orange-clad hippie at Sascha's party, who equate "free love" with a no-strings-attached model of sexual availability. The inability to break out of this circuit of expectation and appropriation in order to articulate her own desire pushes Anne to the brink of despair, and in such moments the film departs from realism to enter the realm of fantasy and myth.

The Mythical Circe

For Anne as a character—and for Ula Stöckl as a filmmaker—classical mythology offers a template for engaging the rage that emerges from unjust power relations and for figuring this rage not as an individual response to injustice but rather as a collective one: in Stöckl's words, as an "archetype of human behavior."[41] As Anne sits on the daybed in Sascha's apartment smoking a cigarette and crying, a cut replaces her tear-stained face with that of Kirke, who appears here for the first time in the film. An extreme close-up of her face marks Kirke as a fantastical character, whose heavy pancake make-up, bright green eyeshadow, and dark eyeliner accentuate her oddball, waiflike looks (fig. 9). Likewise, a marked shift in the pace of the editing, which cuts rapidly back and forth between the two characters, and a sudden costume change for Anne, signal a transition here. Upon seeing Anne, Kirke exclaims, "There you are at last." When Anne taps Kirke on the forehead, Kirke tells her, "I dreamt of you," but Anne responds with a confused look: Whose dream is this, anyway?

Appearances by Kirke punctuate the final two-thirds of *Nine Lives*, where she emerges as a counterpart to Anne, a figment of her imagination or perhaps a doppelgänger. As film scholar Roswitha Mueller puts it, "The power Kirke has is described on two levels—one realistic, one imaginary—which correspond to the ambiguous status of Kirke in the film: it is hard to tell whether Kirke is an actual character or solely exists in [Anne's] mind. . . . The equivocation around Kirke's existential status is an interesting commentary on Stöckl's part on the fluidity between image creation and social positionality."[42] When she enters into the diegesis of *Nine Lives*, this ambiguous character unsettles its established realism, thereby placing into question the ontological status of the film's images and their origins.

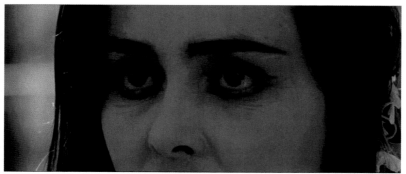

Figure 9. The mythical Kirke (Antje Ellermann) makes her first appearance in the film.

On the one hand, Kirke appears as a character who is empowered to resolve or escape the conundrums of women's desire (and representation) that plague Anne and Katharina—and in this regard she also offers one representational solution to the dilemmas posed by the film itself. As critic Uta Ganschow puts it, "Kirke does not have to search for alternatives: she simply embodies them."[43] Kirke adopts a mode of sexual agency in her interactions with men that appears to be unavailable to the film's less fantastical characters, and she is linked to both the desublimation of trauma and the adoption of creativity and imagination as responses to the stultifying effects of patriarchal socialization on women.

On the other hand, as an invention of Anne's imagination or "an image of an image," Kirke underscores precisely the sense in which women's capacity to imagine is circumscribed by male hegemony over representation.[44] Indeed, she regularly appears in scenarios and in costumes, such as a topless dirndl, that appear to be products of male fantasy—they are especially reminiscent of the popular Bavarian sex films of the period (fig. 10). In *Nine Lives*, these scenarios appropriate and resignify widely circulated erotic images in the context of women's empowerment, but as Mueller points out, they still reflect the "male ideal of the sexually accessible woman of the

Figure 10. Resignifications of male fantasy: Kirke's topless dirndl.

sixties" (64). Kirke, like the other mythological figures that populate Stöckl's oeuvre, thus indexes the ongoing search to find new images of women, their relationships, and their social possibilities, a search that comprises the main narrative force of *Nine Lives*.

When Stöckl began making films in the early 1960s, her search for strong women characters led her to classical mythology, where she found archetypal images of female power and rage that were absent in the cinema. *Antigone*, which Stöckl wrote and shot in Ulm during her first year of film school, offers a seven-minute retelling of Sophocles's *Antigone* and presents an early feminist reclamation of the heroine's challenge to the law and the symbolic order. As Stöckl relates, "I chose Antigone because this Greek figure was a kind of role model for me. We women lacked exemplary models. For me, she was also a metaphor for the revolt against male, patriarchal power."[45] In *The Sleep of Reason*, the character of Dea, based on Medea, serves a similar metaphorical function. A gynecologist and mother of teenage daughters, Dea revolts against heteropatriarchy and capitalism on both individual and collective levels: she spurns her unfaithful husband, who is pursuing an extramarital affair with Dea's medical partner, Johanna, and she fights back against Johanna's father, the powerful drug magnate Erdmann, whose pharmaceutical company profits from the sale of birth-control pills whose negative effects on women's bodies Dea's research has established. As characters drawn from mythology, Antigone, Kirke, and Dea arrive in Stöckl's narratives vested with a special power to flout conformity and adaptation to norms; as such, they are uniquely able to model forms of resistance.[46]

Film scholar Sheila Johnson has pointed out that the appropriation of mythology underpins both the feminist politics of Stöckl's filmmaking and "her approach to form/content unity as aesthetic expression," making it an important vector for her authorial voice.[47] This unity of form and content is evident in the sequence when Kirke first appears in *Nine Lives*, which portrays a puppet show that she and Anne perform with marionettes. The puppet show replays in miniature the gendered dialogs that have comprised the main narrative of the film up until now. As puppet masters, Anne and Kirke both mimic and intervene in these dialogs, highlighting the sense in which individuals are bound by the scripts that circumscribe social interactions and also poking fun at the absurdity of those scripts. Maneuvering a yellow-clad male puppet, Kirke announces that he is prepared to answer any questions posed by the female puppet, who is clothed in a pink princess dress and veil: he will tell her everything! Anne, voicing the princess, responds with her own oft-repeated question, "Do you love me?" Here the script changes when the prince responds, "I love you more than myself . . . I love you so much, I can't say," an answer that Anne never hears from any of the male characters in the main narrative. But then Kirke shifts the terms of engagement again. When Anne's princess follows up with the question, "Am I beautiful?," the prince replies, "I don't want to look at you, I want you to come," and he thrusts his face into her lap, simulating oral sex. She equivocates and pulls away, but then relents and comes closer; as the prince grabs her and lays his whole body on top of hers, pushing her down, she cries, "Please don't!," and he responds, "But don't you want to come?" Anne's princess again responds equivocally, "Yes . . . maybe." "Always maybe," says the prince, disappointed, and the princess responds, "I don't know. . . ." As she manipulates the male marionette, Kirke introduces an overtly erotic dimension into the puppet show that parallels the role she plays in the film as a whole. Whereas Anne's voracious need to be loved and admired suggests the narcissism of her desire, Kirke's repeated question—"Don't you want to come?"—insistently asserts the stakes of sexual liberation. The gendered dialog and body language enacted by the puppets points to the inhibiting role of socialization on women's sexuality, but the princess's protests as she shrinks away from the bold advances of the prince suggest a more difficult impediment to women's sexual emancipation: the trauma of sexual exploitation and abuse.

This trauma is given direct visual expression in a kind of dream-within-the-dream or flashback sequence that interrupts the puppet show. The musical soundtrack that had accompanied the show gives way to complete silence, and a smash cut opens onto a wide shot of children running across a farmyard. In close-up, we see the tear-stained face of one of the children, a girl of about five, clothed in a red plaid skirt and white cardigan sweater with a flowered kerchief on her head. The girl looks on in horror as the farmer uses a large knife to slaughter a hare that is hung up by its feet from a hook on the barn. In a shot/reverse-shot editing rhythm that is unusual for *Nine Lives*, we see the girl's crying face juxtaposed with the jeering figures of the other children, mostly boys, who laugh and point at her, presumably in a rejoinder for her sentimentality regarding the animal's fate (fig. 11). The camera, positioned precisely at the height of the little girl's face, shoots both the farmer and the crowd of boys from a low angle, so that they loom over the frame. In a cutaway shot we see the girl carrying a metal basin, which she places underneath the slaughtered hare. As she walks off, an extreme close-up displays the glistening viscera of the animal's blood-red internal organs piled up in the basin. In a rapid sequence of shots, we again see the farmer carving up the hare, surrounded by the jeering boys, as the girl stands by, tears spilling from her eyes.

In an apparent continuation of this flashback sequence, we now see a man appear at the top of a dark staircase, holding a small girl by the hand. The man carries a candle and the girl carries a doll. Although this girl is younger, about two years old, her costuming in a red plaid skirt and white cardigan sweater suggests that she is the same girl whom we encountered in the previous scene. They descend into the darkness below, and in a rapid montage, we see the doll being set on fire, a metaphor for sexual violence and abuse. As the girl watches in terror, flames engulf the doll, whose bright red skirt

Figure 11. Flashback to childhood trauma: a farmer slaughters a hare as jeering boys look on.

Figure 12. The burning doll as a metaphor for violence against women.

resembles not only her own outfit, but also the costumes worn by the women protagonists of *Nine Lives* (fig. 12).

Insofar as this sequence presents the resurfacing of childhood trauma, with both the hare and the doll appearing as nightmarish stand-ins for the little girl's abuse at the hands of an older man, perhaps a father or grandfather, it is not entirely clear whose perspective or memory is being represented here. Among the miniatures that comprise the patchwork narrative of *Nine Lives*, this sequence stands out: it includes characters and settings we don't encounter elsewhere in the film, and the color and lighting schemes, the old-fashioned clothing, and the presence of a large group of children mark it as dissimilar from other scenes. The metonymy in costuming, however—the red dresses of the doll, the girl, and the women in the film—which is also connected to the scarlet entrails of the slaughtered animal, underscores that the shared experience of violence and exploitation accrues to any and all of them.

This flashback sequence ends with a cut to black and the return of sound. In a direct inversion of the colorful but silent images we have just witnessed—an inversion that compels us to contemplate the implications of the previous scene—the frame remains black for a full seventeen seconds as we listen to the tones of birds chirping, engine noises, and tires on pavement. Eventually, a car's headlights appear in view, we discern the outlines of dark figures, and Katharina's voice returns us to the film's main narrative. Exiting Sascha's apartment in the middle of the night after she has slept with him following the party, Katharina discovers Anne waiting for her by the car and admonishes her not to be miserable: "You wanted me to do as I did." The women's conversation continues the next morning in Katharina's bed, where they discuss the previous evening's events while nursing hangovers. When Anne asks Katharina, "Why did you accept my declaration of war yesterday evening?," Katharina responds, "[I didn't realize you were starting a war]." Another iteration of the film's attention to the conjunctions of war, power, and love, their dialog here addresses how women's rage in the face of their subjugation often fuels competition rather than solidarity. As Anne tells her friend, "When I see your face, I immediately want to hurt you." Subsequently, the women argue about whether it's right to expose their vulnerability to others, with Katharina emphasizing that surrendering oneself to someone else is the only way to discover if one is truly loved. Their dialog circles back to the dilemma to which the mythical Kirke offers one response, the dilemma of women's articulation and expression of desire and creativity in patriarchal society.

Feminist Representation and Documentary Style

The Cat Has Nine Lives stands out for its interventionist approach to the conventions of both narrative cinema and classical realism. Rather than linear plot development, it presents a patchwork of analytical miniatures, and it consistently departs from realist representation, offering counterimages through its incorporation of dreams, flashbacks, and fantasy sequences like those featuring Kirke. Yet the film also archives the moment of its emergence, capturing the historical present of 1968 with spontaneity and originality. Reminiscent of cinema verité, this documentary style, most evident in the central portion of the film, emerged from Stöckl's hands-on, improvisational approach, which led her to shoot scenes in authentic settings with fictional characters—themselves often played by nonprofessional actors—and to go off script to incorporate unexpected events into the film. Stöckl's interventionist style in many ways anticipates Claire Johnston's position that in women's cinema, "ideas derived from the entertainment film ... should inform the political film, and political ideas should inform the entertainment cinema: a two-way process."[48] Indeed, the dialectical interaction between narrative and documentary style in *Nine Lives* presages the significant debates to emerge in feminist film theory in coming decades that often pitted aesthetic experimentation against political immediacy in conceptualizing women's filmmaking practice.

Turning from interpersonal relationships to professional life—yet notably insisting on the imbrication of the private and public spheres in a way that anticipates the feminist motto "the personal is political"—the middle section of *Nine Lives* presents scenes of Stefan, Katharina, and Gabriele at work, while also portraying Anne's explicit renunciation of careerism. Stefan, an airplane engineer, watches a round of test flights for the vertical take-off and landing aircraft (*Senkrechtstarter*) that he helped to design. Subsequently, Katharina conducts a lengthy interview with Gabriele, observing the pop star over several sessions as she learns, arranges, and records the song "The Cat Has Nine Lives." Attending to process—testing an aircraft, recording a song, and writing an article—this sequence further features the negotiations Katharina undertakes with an editor at the magazine where she hopes to publish her profile of Gabriele.

Stöckl has emphasized in interviews the significance of the careers she selected for her figures, noting that it was especially important for Stefan's characterization that his occupation carried particularly masculine, even "macho" associations, in order to highlight the seemingly natural gendering of the professions—a particularly salient topic for women trying to break into the male-dominated film industry.[49] Crucial to her depiction of the gendered professional milieus in which the characters work, Stöckl gained permission to shoot on location at the Dornier Aircraft Works and at a Munich recording studio, and the realistic settings and ad-hoc quality of the footage that resulted plays an important role in the film's aesthetic and political construction.

The remarkable scene in which we see Stefan at work visualizes men's labor in the service of patriarchal culture's militaristic, techno-futurist aspirations. This sequence begins in the domestic space of Stefan's apartment, where he kisses his wife and children goodbye. A striking overhead shot marks the shift from private to public space, framing Stefan's exit onto the street below from the perspective of his family, whom we see in reverse angle waving from the top-floor balcony above. Again from this bird's-eye view, we see Stefan's car maneuver out of its parking space and into the street. A cut to the aircraft he has helped to design, which we see rolling down the runway in a long tracking shot, extends the metonymy between Stefan and motor vehicles, established earlier in the film by a shot of him holding a toy car, and foreshadows the film's final sequence.

An arresting montage follows, portraying actual test flights undertaken by the Dornier Do 31 vertical take-off transport jet, an experimental aircraft that was the subject of much attention in the late 1960s. Under the sign of the Cold War, the West German air force and NATO backed the development of aircraft that would not require airstrips but could be mobilized to take off and land on the Autobahn in the event that airfields came under attack. In *Nine Lives*, the gleaming silver, needle-nosed Do 31 takes off, flies out, and circles back, as crews of technicians and engineers (including Stefan) look on through binoculars from the ground and the control tower. A series of medium shots frames the aircraft in mid-flight; the jump cuts that conjoin these shots, which display the plane from a range of slightly different angles, emphasize the fetishization of this rather phallic machine. Thus, it is all the more surprising, both for the diegetic spectators and for the viewers of the film, when the plane swoops in for a landing only to crash onto the ground in a spectacular belly flop (fig. 13). A reaction shot reveals Stefan's agitation at the pronounced failure of the plane's test flight, before long shots show fire engines, repair trucks, and helicopters speeding to the site of the accident.

Fortuitously, Stöckl had brought two camera teams to the shoot at Dornier: both Mauch and his assistant, Lohmann, captured the incident on film. Lohmann handed over his footage to Dornier officials, but Mauch was quick-witted enough to disguise the fact that

Figure 13. Failed techno-futurist aspirations: the Dornier Do 31 comes in for a crash landing.

he had also been filming. Dornier later offered Stöckl DM 40,000 to cut the whole episode from her film. Her refusal to eliminate the renegade footage proved significant not only for enhancing the film's authenticity but also because it contributes to the broader representation of creativity, process, and making things—including the awkwardness that ensues when these attempts (quite literally) fall flat.

Following the failure of the Do 31's test flight, Stefan discusses the project's ambitions with a group of friends. As he propounds its benefits (reducing noise pollution for city dwellers; limiting the necessity of chopping down forests and pouring concrete for airports), his wife—Magdalena—and another woman look on, exchanging skeptical glances. Someone suggests that, given the probable difficulties in securing subsidies for the project following this failure, the team might want to take it to America, where funding would be easier to obtain, but Stefan objects that it doesn't make sense for a state to invest in a project only to drop it. As he emphasizes, "The idea behind subsidies needs clarifying." This brief conversation echoes the common concerns of West German filmmakers, who similarly looked to the opportunities afforded by Hollywood when struggling to acquire financing for projects in development, a parallel that opens up the topic of commercial considerations in cultural production.

This topic is taken up again in the subsequent scene, which focuses on Katharina's journalistic process—itself subject to the commercial imperative of the media to commodify women's images—as she profiles Gabriele, who in turn balances the market-orientation of the music industry with the creative process of developing and recording a song. Before Gabriele is even introduced as a character in *Nine Lives*, she is presented as a problem of representation, a figure who indexes the rift between feminine artifice and women's subjectivity. Anne is taking a bubble bath while Katharina sits beside the tub applying lotion to her face. In this intimate setting, Anne probes her friend's intentions: "Kathrin, I don't understand you. If you are interested in Gabriele, why not [just] write for the [illustrated] magazines?" But Katharina insists that Gabriele interests her as a person, highlighting the incompatibility of a focus on women's experiences with the sensationalist requirements of mainstream image-making. Anne responds with a critical take, anticipating the many reviews and scholarly treatments of *Nine Lives* that took issue with Stöckl's inclusion of a subplot about a pop star in the film: "I think there are other topics that are more interesting. Don't you think?"

A cut introduces Gabriele, who appears in medium close-up, framed by the green branches of a plant. She sits on a wicker sofa smoking a cigarette as Katharina interviews her, wearing a striking white headband and lots of rings. Gabriele is framed by her living room's decorative wallpaper and surrounded by bouquets of flowers and knickknacks, in a mise-en-scène that amplifies her ornamental quality. It is the tension between Gabriele's performance of femininity and the subject behind this construction, the glamour of the pop star and the labor involved in both the creation of music and the performance of the self, that interests Katharina within the diegesis of the film, a metatextual plot line that resonates with Ula Stöckl's own attention to women's representation in *Nine Lives*. Film scholar Temby Caprio has aptly summarized the importance of Gabriele to Stöckl's project: "Gabriele's character and, in fact, her career offer the film's most legible meditation on female subjectivity and the traditional position of woman in film culture as 'image' and not agent. . . . More than the sum of her surface image and her narcissistic reflection on this image, Gabriele as played by Stroh is also a cipher of female performativity."[50] As Caprio goes on to suggest, Katharina likewise occupies a complex position relative to the film's metacritical discourse on women and film: she is both a consumer-fan who is visibly fascinated by Gabriele and takes pleasure in watching her perform, and a journalist who negotiates over the production of Gabriele's public image.

Echoing the previous sequence's focus on financial considerations in the creative process of developing new aircraft, Gabriele responds to Katharina's opening question about what kinds of songs she most likes to perform by stating bluntly, "What counts is that it's a commercial success. Then it wins [over] the audience." Katharina probes the tensions epitomized by Gabriele with a series of questions about the relationship between public and private life, asking whether professional fulfillment constitutes happiness for the star and whether it is because of her career that she is unmarried. Following a long monologue in which Gabriele explains why marriage is incompatible with her professional life, a series of close-ups shows Katharina and Gabriele laughing uproariously. Both women are framed in profile, their faces juxtaposed with images of women pinned up on the wall behind them: colorful pictures torn from the pages of women's magazines as well as black-and-white glamour shots of Gabriele herself. Cracking up, Gabriele tells Katharina, "You've got to laugh! It's no good always being serious," and then she turns to the wall behind her and begins to critique the photos of herself that are hanging there (fig. 14): "Lord! Look at these pictures! I'm such a forbidding beauty in them. I'm never supposed to laugh." This mutual

Figure 14. Gabriele (Heidi Stroh) makes fun of her own image.

laughter at women's representation in dominant culture constitutes a moment of solidarity and self-awareness within the conversation and the film that briefly punctures the facade of gendered performance and image creation. The subsequent dialog once more highlights the artifice of Gabriele's performance of femininity: she tells Katharina that she's attracted to unusual men (Jesus is the type of man she could fall in love with); that she doesn't find herself beautiful; and that women usually hate her until they get to know her—clichés that confirm the narcissism of this pop icon.

While the interview scene thus reflects and interrogates both the decorative role of women in popular culture and the artifice of gender performance more broadly, subsequent scenes attend to the other side of the coin: women's creativity and their role in the process of making things. In the evening, Katharina accompanies Gabriele to a rehearsal with Erwin Halletz that takes place at a residential home filled with modern furniture, green plants, and a white piano. A well-known composer of *Schlager* songs and film music who makes a cameo appearance here, Halletz cowrote "The Cat Has Nine Lives" with Max Colpet.[51] Halletz offers Gabriele two possible arrangements of the song: a more rhythmic, jazz-inspired variant; and a more listener-friendly, commercial variant, which Gabriele chooses. In an extended musical interlude, Gabriele learns this arrangement of the song, practicing different phrasings, discussing which words to stress, and considering options for a bridge. As Katharina looks on, occasionally offering a suggestion or affirmation, Gabriele negotiates tempo and intonation with Halletz, and the two sing lengthy passages of the song.

An abrupt cut places us in the editorial office of the magazine where Katharina hopes to publish her profile of Gabriele. Accompanied by her friend Manfred (Hartmut Kirste), Katharina pitches her story to an editor in a pivotal sequence that condenses the film's attention to women's representation (fig. 15). Telling the editor about Gabriele, Katharina exclaims, "She's a ready-made star,"

She's a ready-made star.

Figure 15. Metacritical discourse on women's representation: Katharina's pitch to her editor.

but he expresses concern that the piece will simply function as a promotional advertisement. Katharina has a different concern: while the editor pushes her to find a novel angle for the story, Katharina reflects on the position of the journalist in an era before feminist publishing enabled a more critical form of reporting about women's personal and professional lives. She wonders aloud about the ethics of her participatory approach to interviewing Gabriele: "I rallied her on, acted [enthusiastically], said: it'll be an earworm! But now I've got to know her and have become interested in her as a person. She's become trusting, has confided in me, taken me along, now I feel like a traitor." Disregarding her concerns and failing to comprehend the critical approach that Katharina proposes, the editor again asks, "How will you sell the story?" The phone rings, and when he picks up the receiver the editor speaks to the writer on the other end of the line about "a kind of pop-comedy. The love they sing of, the love they dance for, et cetera! Youngsters rebel against tradition, society, and bourgeois morality. How about it?" The editor's enthusiasm for this piece contrasts sharply with his skepticism about Katharina's project, which he characterizes in highly reductive terms: "Well, I still don't really see the story. It's half biography, half sociology of the star, and half a tearjerker about a girl. As soon as we do this, well, we're aiding [the song's] success." Whereas the editor is enthusiastic about publishing a (rather clichéd) story about young rebels—presumably men—his patience for clichés does not extend to the portrait of Gabriele, which he pejoratively labels a tearjerker.

Katharina's dialog with the editor throws into sharp relief both the commercial media's response to the zeitgeist of 1968 and its gender politics in the era before second-wave feminism's development of a counterpublic sphere. Journalism and editorial work would become a focal point of feminist German cinema in subsequent years, perhaps most famously in Margarete von Trotta's *Marianne and Juliane* (*Die bleierne Zeit*, 1981), a film that explores two sisters' divergent paths to effecting political change—Marianne embraces armed resistance, while Juliane works as the editor of a feminist magazine. Von Trotta's film emphasizes the stark contrast between the spectacular tactics of the urban guerrilla movement and the arduous process of negotiation that characterized feminist approaches to reporting and editing, a process that *Nine Lives* already makes visible.

Katharina's visit to the editor in *Nine Lives* strongly foreshadows a similar scene in Sander's *Redupers*, when protagonist Edda Chiemnyjewski likewise encounters a dismissive and unsympathetic magazine editor who refuses to comprehend the project she is pitching about women's representation. In fact, the "pop-comedy" described by Katharina's editor sounds awfully similar to *The Cat Has Nine Lives*, itself a tale of rebellion "against tradition, society, and bourgeois reality" replete with song and dance. Yet the editor's dismissive response to Katharina's representation of Gabriele—a portrait that emphasizes the subjectivity of a woman artist in tension with her public image—dovetails with the negative reception of *Nine Lives* as an "unserious" film about women.

Following the film's premiere in Mannheim, viewers not only failed to comprehend its focus on women but also were flabbergasted that it did not include any male protagonists. As Stöckl recalled in 1977: "I was accused of making a film in which men don't appear at all. People were constantly asking me if I could imagine making a film like this with men instead. Apparently men felt completely left out of this film! And of course I was also faulted for portraying totally gratuitous things—the aesthetics of the film made people crazy, they found it horribly trendy."[52] In the absence of a theoretical discourse about feminist aesthetics, Stöckl's unmasking of the tensions and contradictions inherent in conventions of women's representation was misperceived, even misunderstood. Whereas conservative critics indicted the film's attention to women's emancipation, critics on the left faulted it for failing to offer a vision of female solidarity. At the same time, the pop style of *Nine Lives* was conflated in the public imagination with its focus on women's lives, with both dimensions of the film viewed as superficial. Even feminist critics struggled to comprehend Stöckl's resignification of clichés: writing in 1977, Claudia Lenssen compared the film's floral imagery to "the romanticized photos of girls familiar from [teen magazines] that can be found today in o.b. tampon commercials."[53] The humor and irony of *Nine Lives*, and its engagement with pleasure and desire, contrasted sharply with both the earnest films of the early NGC and the political immediacy of emergent feminist cinema. Yet this humor is crucial to the film's emphasis on the absurdity of culturally prescribed gender roles.

This absurdity is nowhere more evident than in the scenes of *Nine Lives* featuring Sascha, including his conversation with Katharina at a beer garden where she meets him after her editorial pitch. Emphasizing the intersections of Katharina's private and professional lives, this conversation returns to the topic of marriage as a normative horizon of expectation for women when Sascha rather hilariously offers to solve Katharina's problems by marrying her. Although (or perhaps because) they have recently slept together, the awkwardness of their conversation is registered by the fact that Sascha and Katharina use the formal mode of address; Sascha's patronizing and obfuscating tendencies, as well as his propensity to explain things to women, are again on full display.

Katharina explains the ethical dilemma that she faces as a journalist because of her tendency to approach her subjects emotionally and her struggle with craftmanship and technical know-how, since she lacks formal training. Like the editor before him, Sascha utterly fails to respond to the substance of Katharina's concerns, instead asking her, "Might it be that your confidence doesn't come from academic studies, for which it's too late now, but from the human side, like, for example, from marriage? It needn't be formal marriage, it could be a liaison that offers you a certain security. . . ." The camera cuts to an extreme close-up of Sascha's face as Katharina pointedly asks, "What are you actually getting at with your insistence that I need a partner?" Sascha responds defensively: "I thought I'd made myself sufficiently clear. Now you only need insert the person's name. Whether it's called a marriage or not isn't. . . . That's a secondary issue. *I'd like to marry you*, but it needn't necessarily be a marriage. There are intermediate solutions. So, well. . . ." We see both characters framed in a two-shot, their faces partially obscured in shadow, their half-empty beer glasses on the table in the foreground. Fidgeting with her glasses, Katharina stares concentratedly at her lap, refusing eye contact with Sascha, as he concludes his proposal: "I'm pretty sure that the problems you speak of can best be solved in this fashion." An abrupt cut shows the couple in reverse angle, the camera positioned behind Katharina so that we see the empty tables stretching out around them in a shot that presages the social isolation a marriage with Sascha would portend, as Katharina asks him, "What if I don't love you?" (fig. 16). Sascha pontificates about marital love, but Katharina cuts him off, an interruption that is underscored by an abrupt shift of camera angle, so that we see her centered in the frame as she explains why she must refuse Sascha's proposal: "I repeatedly have the experience of trying to change things by participating in something with all my strength and all my determination. . . . I try to find something new

What if I don't love you?

Figure 16. Envisioning the social isolation of marriage: Katharina rejects Sascha's proposal.

without even knowing what it might be. So [I can't marry]." A close-up shows Sascha's face as Katharina, refusing to let him intercede, puts it to him directly: "I have to say no." Katharina emphasizes how her quest for alternative imaginaries and structural change must be mutually exclusive with a marital bond, in a scene that underscores the film's broader critique of the constraints placed on women by the institution of marriage and also neatly deconstructs the marriage plot as narrative resolution.

While Katharina seeks change by emancipating herself from traditional relationships in order to pursue a writing career, Anne renounces the professional realm altogether. In a companion scene to the previous one, Anne and Manfred visit a swimming pool, where he begins a conversation with her about what she does for a living. "You have to do something," he tells her, just as the heavens open and rain begins to pour. At first, Anne and Manfred take shelter from the storm under an awning, but then we see Anne, in a confirmation of her free-spiritedness, belly flopping into the pool, laughing at herself, and taking a swim in the pouring rain. As in earlier scenes where she floated in a pond and took a bubble bath, Anne is submerged in water here, aligning her with the unconscious, fantastical, and erotic powers of the element.[54] After she swims, the conversation resumes as Anne proclaims: "I don't want a career at all. I reject all forms of career. I won't play along. If you do something, you play along. I'd rather perish than play along. I work only for my phone, my apartment, and so on. But for nothing else in the world." We see Anne in close-up, as she declares, "I can do something new every day!" Echoing Katharina's previous statement to Sascha ("I try to find something new without even knowing what it might be"), Anne's declaration emphasizes that, even as they take different approaches to the search for alternatives, both women share a commitment to emancipation from prescribed norms.

A smash cut takes us to the studio where Gabriele is recording "The Cat Has Nine Lives." Unfolding almost like a music video— the diegetic soundtrack consists only of the song, and no dialog is audible—this miniature follows the action as studio musicians lay down the track while Katharina looks on. Gabriele arrives, dressed in a frilly transparent blouse and smoking a cigarette in a holder. As she practices the song, a cutaway montage sequence portrays Gabriele, now dressed in a black beret and feather boa, posing for the camera and offering a series of flirtatious facial expressions that reflect the song lyrics ("But when someone strokes me, spoils and compliments me, I am the sweetest, most enchanting creature in the world"), a sequence that invokes the artifice and self-fashioning of Gabriele's performance of femininity. Alluding again to the significant work involved in this performance, the film here depicts the negotiations between the star and composer Halletz while they record, emphasizing the laborious process of getting the song right (fig. 17) as Gabriele struggles with finding the right key. This sequence concludes not with the final polished product but on a provisional, open note, as the team listens critically and Halletz makes suggestions for another take.

The documentary-style immediacy and improvisational quality of this scene contribute significantly to the film's authenticity, but it

Figure 17. Creative labors: Gabriele records "The Cat Has Nine Lives" with composer Erwin Halletz.

became the subject of controversy when Heidi Stroh filed suit against Ula Stöckl, claiming that the film's negative portrayal of Gabriele— and in particular the inclusion of footage documenting her failure to sing well—was defamatory. While the suit was eventually dismissed, it is worth mentioning here chiefly because it highlights once more the tendency to misunderstand Stöckl's project in *Nine Lives* (a tendency that, as we have seen, is itself metacritically addressed throughout this portion of the film). Whereas it is unusual for an actor to accuse a filmmaker of defamation in the portrayal of a fictional character, Stroh—herself a former nightclub singer—evidently perceived the film's depiction of Gabriele as documentary in nature. The film's formal experimentation and defiance of conventional generic categories repeatedly engendered such misapprehensions. As Caprio puts it, "Audiences, it seems, were not ready to conceive of women's experiences in unconventional cinematic terms."[55] Critics too, tended to dwell on the improvisational, nonfictional components of the film (neglecting its highly constructed dream and fantasy sequences) or to simply lump it together with other documentary-style works perceived as socially critical. In his 1978 history of German film since 1960, for instance, Ulrich Gregor devotes whole chapters to a range of young German auteur filmmakers (all men), while including women filmmakers only in an umbrella chapter devoted to realists and documentarians, further contributing to the feminization of these forms.[56]

The tendency to (willfully) misperceive its formal aims notwithstanding, *The Cat Has Nine Lives* contributes to the development of a critical feminist film aesthetics precisely through its collaging and juxtaposition of documentary and narrative elements. Like other women-directed European films of the 1960s—including Agnès Varda's *Cleo from 5 to 7* (France, 1961), Lina Wertmüller's *The Lizards* (Italy, 1963), Mai Zetterling's *Loving Couples* (Sweden, 1964), and Vera Chytilová's *Daisies* (Czechoslovakia, 1966)—Stöckl's film aims to make realism visible, even to rupture realistic representation from within, and especially realist conventions of portraying women.

In one of the film's most striking collage sequences, Anne joins an antiwar demonstration. Shot during an actual protest march in Munich, this sequence captures the countercultural and anti-establishment spirit of 1968 and also suggested an autofictional dimension by registering Stöckl's own somewhat vexed relationship to the student movement. The sequence opens on an image of Anne, clothed in a bright yellow trench coat and a scarf in the *Tricolore* motif of the French flag, marching in step with other young people through the streets. In long shot, we see Anne centered in the frame, surrounded by placards and banners, one of which reads "Vietnam: Today Bombs and Gas, Tomorrow Atom Bombs?" (fig. 18). A montage portrays the marching demonstrators, who chant in unison, and close-ups of signs display Martin Luther King Jr., Rudi Dutschke, and a Vietnamese mother holding a dead child. Handmade posters demand disarmament, peace, and the US withdrawal from Vietnam. A bright red banner plaintively asks, "Yesterday Jews, today students, and tomorrow?" As footage of the protest unspools, Anne, in voiceover, describes the general strike initiated by French students in May 1968 and her fear of violence at demonstrations like this one because of a head injury she sustained at the hands of police during a Paris protest. Yet she has not let this fear impede her

Figure 18. Documenting 1968: Anne joins a protest against the Vietnam War.

participation in the movement because, as she puts it, "There are things one has to do." The disjuncture between Anne's voiceover and the visual track fractures the naturalized relation between sound and image here, drawing attention to the combination of narrative and documentary modes. Following the protest, Anne sits at a café with a fellow protester, a man likewise dressed in yellow, who wonders why she is attending a march in Germany. Anne explains that she happens to be visiting from France. When she reveals that she isn't a student, he asks her whether she even knows what the protest is about, and Anne wryly replies, "Of course I do. We are bringing about world revolution!" Channeling Stöckl's own experiences as a woman and nonstudent sympathetic to the cause, this dialog illustrates the elitist and patronizing tendencies of men in the student movement, a topic memorably addressed by Helke Sander in her magnum opus, *The Subjective Factor* (*Der subjective Faktor*, 1981), a film that likewise provocatively combines fiction and documentary in its representation of the caesura of 1968 in German history and culture.

Alternative Imaginaries

Both its vexed reception history and comparisons to Sander's later feminist films help to elucidate how *The Cat Has Nine Lives* anticipates subsequent aesthetic and political developments in ways that could only become clear in retrospect. In this regard, the film enables a broader consideration of deferred time and feminist futurity. As feminist philosopher Elizabeth Grosz reminds us,

> In addressing . . . the future of thought, it is not possible to leap out of our own time and into the reality of the future-made present. At best, what we have access to are the most complex and cutting-edge discourses and practices (political, scientific, and artistic), those that seek out a future, those that take risks, that welcome innovation and transformation. Although these may not prove to be indices to predicting the future of thought, they do provide lines of flight, directions of movement that are *virtual in the present*, laden with potentialities, and that thus have some impetus or force in engendering a future that is different from what we have now.[57]

As Grosz goes on to suggest, encountering forgotten or misunderstood historical texts can "revivify . . . the past as a mode of access to or anticipation of a future yet to come" (157). Grosz's notion of revivification helps to conceptualize feminist time as a mode of archiving the future, one to which the time-based and utopian artistic forms of cinefeminism make a particularly significant contribution.

Writing in 1980, film scholar Renate Möhrmann contended that "Despite the shortcomings of a first film, *The Cat Has Nine Lives* was certainly ahead of its time, not least in its rejection of the dominant narrative realism of the 1960s."[58] And in 1992, journalist and filmmaker Christa Maerker recalled,

> When Ula showed her first film *The Cat Has Nine Lives*, something happened to me that I couldn't explain. The feminist movement didn't yet exist, but here was a feminist film. It was Ula's film, and no one knew how to deal with

> it. . . . I only knew that something revolutionary had unfolded before my very eyes, but it couldn't be named, because the vocabulary wasn't there for it. This consciousness couldn't be named. But something was just being awakened, and the film had a great deal to do with this awakening.[59]

As Möhrmann and Maerker suggest, the feminist futurity of Stöckl's film was already *virtually* legible, in Grosz's sense, amid the transformative spirit of 1968, and this futurity was especially evident in the film's form. Indeed, the final sections of *Nine Lives*, in which its collage aesthetic emerges most powerfully, are rife with counterpoints to dominant heteropatriarchal constructs that imaginatively rupture normative regimes of gender and sexuality.

Anne's proclamation "We are bringing about world revolution!" is directly followed by a scene that documents the movement for antiauthoritarian education that was one of the chief focal points of West German second-wave feminism. Together with Sascha, Anne, and a few other adults, Katharina sits on the floor of a day care and passionately advocates for allowing young children to express their sexuality in an uninhibited fashion, since "auto-eroticism makes you more independent of your partner" and because a nonrepressive upbringing enhances the likelihood that children will grow up freer and happier. Katharina joins a group of bare-bottomed children who place pillows between their legs and ride them around the room like horses in a play session that promotes ease with nudity and self-pleasure, a powerful sex-positive moment (fig. 19). Later, Katharina embraces this playful spirit with Stefan, flirting with him from her car when she notices him driving next to her and bringing him back to her apartment, where the two amuse themselves in bed with paper fortune tellers that Katharina has crafted.

A close-up displays a museum vitrine containing a bejeweled golden statuette of St. George and his horse. A woman, whom we recognize as Anne, circles the vitrine; her reflection is visible

Figure 19. The movement for antiauthoritarian education: Katharina promotes sex-positive play.

in its shiny glass, superimposed on the statue. In a striking shot underscoring her duality as subject and object of the gaze, Anne's face appears split in two as she peers into the glass, bats her eyelids, and smiles (fig. 20a). She continues to circle the sculpture, examining it from every possible angle and pressing her face against the case in an attempt to perceive its fine details, before she steps back and looks over her shoulder to see if anyone else has noticed the imprints left by her mouth and nose on the glass (fig. 20b). Positioning Anne as the diegetic spectator, whose haptic, tactile mode of observation literally smudges the transparent surface that separates her from the work of art, this scene calls attention to forms of mediation between viewer and object of vision, making us aware of the cinematic apparatus and especially of the screen. Later, Anne meets Katharina outside the museum, and the two sit under a very large statue—also of a horse and rider—as Anne lays down eight cards, inviting Katharina to play a matching game. Katharina picks two cards, and Anne turns them over, revealing reproductions of St. George; when she turns over the rest of the cards, we see that they are all identical reproductions of the image, underscoring this sequence's meditation on questions of originality, authenticity, and multiplicity raised by the technical mediation of cinema.

Figures 20a–b. Haptic visuality: Anne as subject and object of the gaze.

An abrupt cut initiates an extended sequence marking the reappearance of Anne's fantastical counterpart Kirke. Although this figure was introduced earlier, it is only now that we hear Anne speak of her directly. Anne and Katharina lie in the dark, their bodies partially obscured and their faces only briefly illuminated by the light of the matches that Anne repeatedly strikes. Speaking in French, Anne tells Katharina, "She's a woman who's very strange and wonderful." When Katharina asks if Kirke is married, Anne replies "No. Sometimes. No one knows. It's unknowable. She's a nymphomaniac, a mythomaniac, a kleptomaniac. She does just what she likes. She's a kleptomaniac when she wants, she can even blow up the Eiffel Tower." The dark image is abruptly replaced with an extreme close-up of Kirke. The roar of the audio track underscores the film's departure from realism, and cold frontal lighting intensifies the appearance of Kirke's fine mustache as she looks directly into the camera, which pans down from her face to her bare décolletage. Integral to the film's depiction of alternative imaginaries, Kirke blurs masculine and feminine attributes, embodying a nonnormative gender presentation that confounds the gender binary; her sexual agency and overt eroticism likewise queer this character. Anne's concluding statement about Kirke—"*That's what I call a woman*"—accentuates the film's emphasis on the contingency, fluidity, and performativity of gender and sexuality and its concomitant destabilization of the category "woman," anticipating the trenchant critiques of poststructuralist feminist and queer theory.

Holding a large bouquet of purple irises, Katharina and Stefan stand in the hallway of a hospital ward. With a loud creak, a door opens to reveal Kirke, who welcomes the visitors into her room. All three characters sit on the bed, and Kirke offers to read aloud a story she has written about a childhood memory of playing a game called "ride-the-pig" on the farm where she grew up. As she speaks, Stefan places his hand inside Kirke's blouse, a gesture that is emphasized by a two-shot that dwells on his tactile stroking of her breast. Proclaiming in a provocative tone, "I'd sometimes get *incredibly* dirty," Kirke laughs with pleasure at Stefan's erotic stroking. Now Katharina appears holding a sword, dressed as St. George, in a meadow filled with white and yellow flowers, where Stefan and Kirke lie in an embrace. Dissonant music plays as the camera repeatedly pans across the pastoral landscape, where the figures appear and disappear, emphasizing the dreamlike nature of this vision. In close-up, we see Anne, who laughs out loud at her own dream, telling Kirke, "I pictured Katharina to myself, she was protecting the lovers." Fantasizing about Katharina in drag, and overlaying her affinity with St. George as a figure who represents the triumph of good over evil onto her previous refusal to sanction Stefan's infidelity, this vision suggests Anne's increasing openness to rethinking sexual norms.

This rethinking is encapsulated by the crucial sequence that follows, one that presages feminist philosophy's interest, as Elizabeth Grosz has formulated it, in "the question of how to engender and stimulate not only new political practices, but above all, new thought, new modes of conceptualization, new theories and models adequate to the complexity and hitherto unrepresented qualities and characteristics of women, the feminine, and sexual difference."[60] Katharina appears before a tribunal of older women who challenge her to find an alternative to the institution of marriage. In close-up, her face appears drenched in sweat, and her voiceover suggests how hard it is to break from culturally ingrained practices: "The Indians of Chichicastenango do what they have learned. [We do what we have learned]. Few peoples can do more than what they have learned." A montage of women's faces scrutinize Katharina, who appears unnerved, on the verge of crying, as the voiceover continues, "*We can only imagine that which already exists*" (fig. 21a). "Nonmarriage, that doesn't exist," the voiceover proclaims, "Nor does an alternative to marriage." Now visibly weeping, Katharina embodies a somatic representation of the impasse enunciated by the voiceover. While we recognize this as Katharina's voice, the formal construction of the scene severs her speech from her body. We never see Katharina's lips move, whereas the women who occupy the wood-paneled courtroom—a generation of war widows—gesticulate and pontificate so that the soundtrack seems to be emanating from their mouths. Abruptly, the voiceover ends, though the women's mouths keep moving. The final, arresting image in this scene depicts an older woman centered in the frame, one lens of her glasses clouded over, a literal portrayal of the thwarted eyesight that *Nine Lives*'s kaleidoscopic visions seek to liberate (fig. 21b). In the collage-style aesthetic construction of this scene, devices of fragmentation abound, rupturing the coherence

Figures 21a–b. Imagining alternatives to the impasse of heteropatriarchy: Katharina appears before a tribunal of older women.

of sound, image, and spatiotemporal registers and destabilizing conventional cinematic representation. Even as this scene depicts on a narrative level the impasse of heteropatriarchy, it figures on a formal level a way out of that impasse through its transgression of cinematic norms.

We return to Anne and Kirke, who are framed in a two-shot. Both women hold flowers, and Kirke swings in a white hammock suspended from two trees (fig. 22). When Anne asks about her relationship to Stefan, Kirke responds, "We have a lot of fun together," and an extended sequence depicts their erotic encounter.

Figure 22. The floral fantasies of Anne and Kirke.

Figure 23. Caricaturing male fantasy: Stefan surrounded by dirndl-clad women.

While this fantasy first seems to originate from Kirke's perspective, a shift is marked by Anne's appearance within the scene, and soon all of the film's women characters—including Gabriele, Katharina, and Magdalena—appear, dressed in pink and brown dirndls (fig. 23).

Insofar as the costuming and mise-en-scène replicate the visual vocabulary of 1960s-era Bavarian sex films, Kirke's imagination of a nonphallocentric form of eroticism, visualized through Stefan's repeated stroking of her breasts, seems to verge into the realm of male fantasy here. The static tableau of dirndl-clad women, however,

this scene. Discarding the notion of women's competition for men's attention, Anne again envisions an act of murderous violence against Stefan when she suffocates him with a pillow.

Returning to the diegetic narrative, Anne sits on the bed while Manfred pulls his sweater over her head and then ties its arms around her, a playful image but one that also symbolizes the straitjacket of heteronormative desire. Anne tells Manfred that she's sad, and he tries to cheer her up by drawing a picture, a cartoonish representation of Anne as a mermaid. While he draws, Anne sucks on and eats daisies, and then she covers Manfred's drawing with flowers, pressing the blooms into the mermaid's groin—as if harnessing the erotic power of plants—before pulling Manfred onto the bed and kissing him. As they kiss, Anne repeats her longstanding refrain, "Do you love me?" Like all the other men in *Nine Lives*, Manfred demurs. But in the only instance of male voiceover in the entire film, we hear his voice explain: "If you've waited so long for a girl like Anne, when the moment comes you're worn out." Manfred's explanation emphasizes the exhaustion induced by normative gender and sexual regimes for men as well as women.

In the optically rich and haptically suggestive scene that follows, *Nine Lives* offers an alternative to the impasse of heteropatriarchy by returning to plant life as a figure of desire and autoeroticism (figs. 28 a–b). Anne, who wears a vibrant red pullover, stands in the middle of a field filled with yellow rapeseed flowers in spectacular bloom. As the camera moves in closer, circling around her, Anne begins to strip the leaves off the stalks of the rapeseed plants, leaving only the blossoms, which she inserts into her mouth and voraciously eats. Soaring camera movements accompanied by an ecstatic soundtrack—featuring a sole female voice rhapsodizing in a style reminiscent of throat singing— figure the rapture of Anne's communion with the vegetal world. The music subsides, and the diegetic humming of bugs and birdsong accompanies Anne as she continues to lick and suck the rapeseed blooms and tuck them into her hair. Anne's polymorphous play with

Figures 28a–b. Anne's rapturous communion with the vegetal world.

plants resignifies the decorative, ornamental function of women in classical cinema, disrupting women's objectification and asserting an alternative model of eroticism that we might retrospectively understand as a form of ecosexuality.

Material-feminist and queer-environmental theory has emphasized our ecological entanglements with the nonhuman, including the animal, the vegetal, and the elemental, entanglements that unsettle human claims to autonomous subjectivity, individualist notions of the self, and the transcendence of the human as such. Feminist critic Stacy Alaimo's influential conception of trans-corporeality, for example, accentuates "the imbrication of human bodies not only with each other, but with non-human creatures and physical landscapes."[61] Redefining the human as material, trans-corporeality entails "a critique, subversion, or evasion of the dominant modes of representation and the gendered scenarios of visibility" (18) that resonates with the thoroughgoing destabilization of dominant cinematic language in Stöckl's film.

In her ecological analysis of naked protests, Alaimo touts sex-positive feminism—which promotes the reclaiming of all bodies for pleasure and advocates for the exposure of flesh as a mode of empowerment—as a primary locus for the expression of trans-corporeality. Indeed, nonnormative sexual practices have increasingly been taken up in feminist and queer ecological thought as figures for reconceptualizing environmentalism. Queer theorist Sarah Ensor offers the practice of cruising as an "unexpected model for a new ecological ethic," arguing that cruising represents a form of intimacy that is nondirected, ambient, and impersonal, an experience of desire that is notably indifferent to personal identity. [62] As such, she writes, "ecological entanglement resembles the queer relationality of cruising far more than it does the other (more normative) relational paradigms to which we so often analogize it" (151). Alaimo and Ensor underscore how dominant ecological discourses have positioned environmental stewardship as an ethical practice that is predicated on reproductive futurity, chaste restraint, or the common good, evident in concepts like "the seventh generation"; "leave no trace"; and "one earth, one future." By contrast, their work highlights how the alternative models of relationality, intimacy, and care offered by queer, polymorphous, and polyamorous sex can resignify environmentalism as a practice not of "conserving or sustaining present ways of life, but rather [of] rupturing or annihilating norms."[63]

Conceptualizing earth stewardship and eroticism as intertwined practices, the movement for ecosexuality playfully literalizes this feminist-queer vision of environmental ethics. The movement's most famous proponents, feminist sexologist Annie Sprinkle and her wife, artist and filmmaker Beth Stephens, proclaim in their Ecosex Manifesto: "We make love with the earth. We are aquaphiles, teraphiles, pyrophiles and aerophiles. We shamelessly hug trees, massage the earth with our feet, and talk erotically to plants. . . . We are polymorphous and pollen-amorous. . . . We hold these truths to be self evident; that we are all part of, not separate from, nature. Thus all sex is ecosex."[64] Sprinkle and Stephens overtly denaturalize received conceptions of nature, unsettling heteronormative and patriarchal discourses that determine which bodies, roles, and practices are considered un/natural. The florid performances of promiscuity and pollen-amory featured in Stöckl's film likewise call into question the link between woman and nature, while also expanding conceptions of sex, sexuality, and sexual identity.

Endings

The pollen-amory of her play with plants appears in stark contrast to the subsequent sequence in which Anne, wearing a yellow trench coat reminiscent of the rapeseed flowers, sits on a park bench and gorges herself on candy and chocolates. Grasping a handful of brightly-colored lollipops, she plucks bonbons from a box and stuffs them in her mouth. Extreme close-ups of her lips and of the chocolate box portray the grotesquery of this gluttonous consumption, highlighted by the way that the suckers she wipes across her lips resemble processed and denatured flowers (fig. 29). Recalling the sign for candy and flowers in the opening sequence of the film, this final fantasy sequence emphasizes the destructive qualities of capitalist regimes of consumption, especially for women.

Underscoring the film's critique of beauty, Anne stands in front of a mirror examining herself. Though this is the first time in the film we see her reflection in a mirror, this splitting of Anne's image recalls the many instances of doubling throughout *Nine Lives*. Katharina

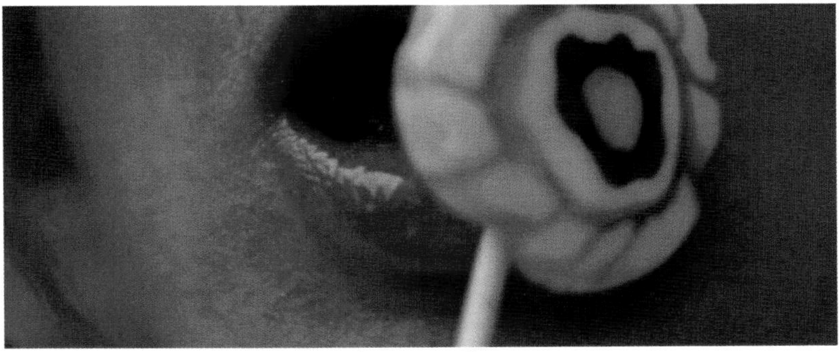

Figure 29. Destructive consumption and the critique of beauty.

enters the frame, and the two women's images join in the mirror. Katharina asks Anne to close her eyes, and in a gesture conventionally performed by a man she places a necklace with a heart-shaped pendant and jewel around Anne's neck. The women's symbolic (re) union, underscored by the fact that they both wear white dresses, is consolidated by a kiss and an embrace. Anne's subsequent departure, from Munich and from the film itself, is accompanied by a reprisal of the opening song, "Fleurs de Vacances," whose final lyrics—"I shall be the flower of your holidays / Open my petals / Take me"—offer a fitting caption to the nascent queerness of this sequence.

Nine Lives does not conclude with the union of Anne and Katharina, however. After she leaves the train station, Katharina meets up with Stefan, and we see the couple having sex. Katharina's face appears in close-up as she sizes up her lover, a sympathetic assessment summarized in voiceover: "If I were to describe him, I'd say his face is a bit crooked. His hairline is lower on the left. And when he turns up his collar, he looks like Chopin." A cut places us inside a car, recalling the film's opening scene of Katharina in the driver's seat, but this time Stefan is at the wheel. A male friend sits in the passenger seat, the road stretching out ahead of them as they drive. In the brief dialog that follows, the two men discuss the possibility of achieving happiness in marriage. Stefan rather ironically asserts that he has to maintain a positive view of the promise of happiness that marriage offers. His friend, however, concludes, "Perhaps you're right, but what we have to watch out for is a[n affirmation] of happiness, *a false love of beginnings.*" At this, the film abruptly cuts to black, concluding with a statement that—even as it gives men the final word—aptly summarizes the circular logic of heteropatriarchy, in which the film's characters remain ensnared.

Although it underscores this circularity, *The Cat Has Nine Lives* also articulates a radically anticipatory stance by rupturing sexual and cinematic norms to begin the process of imagining what doesn't yet exist. This radical vision is expanded in Stöckl's subsequent film, *Tales of the Dumpster Kid* (1969–71), which she wrote and codirected with Edgar Reitz. Again starring Kristine de Loup, *Tales of the Dumpster Kid* comprises a fantastical series of twenty-five short films about a genderless child who emerges full-grown from a placenta that has been discarded in a dumpster outside the maternity ward of a hospital. The dumpster kid enters the world without awareness of social constructs of gender and sexuality. She defies the attempts of various institutions to impose a normative female identity on her, and she experiments with a broad array of sexual practices. We see her making balloons out of condoms, trying out a range of sex toys including a strap-on dildo, and masturbating by walking through a field of grass with no underwear, a next-level vision of Stöckl's pollen-amorous utopia in *Nine Lives.*

Tales of the Dumpster Kid offers a radical vision not only in its depiction of sex and gender but also in its narrative form: audiences voted prior to screenings on the preferred order in which the shorts were to be projected. This participatory format enacted an analog precursor to the interactive storytelling now associated with digital media, one that resulted in a nonlinear mode of narration that disrupted dominant conventions of representation along multiple vectors. In form and content, *Tales of the Dumpster Kid* rejects both narrative teleology and normative constructions of psychosexual development. Notably, this film experiment was in many ways enabled by the "failure" of *Nine Lives*. Unable to finance a second narrative feature, Stöckl embraced collaborative authorship, a DIY filmmaking aesthetic, and a low-budget style not beholden to conventions of continuity, order, or sequence. The foreclosure of a present in sequence with the past, then, opened onto a different modality of being and becoming for Stöckl, realized in the intertwining of dissonant genders, sexualities, and temporalities in films that, still today, anticipate a future that is yet to come.

Among these, *The Cat Has Nine Lives* occupies a unique status. The aesthetic and political project first articulated by Ula Stöckl in 1968 laid the groundwork for the emergence of cinefeminism and presaged the artistic forms and critical interrogations taken up by feminist films and feminist film theory in the 1970s and 1980s. More than fifty years after it debuted, *The Cat Has Nine Lives* remains remarkably relevant to contemporary feminism, offering a resonant approach to revivifying the search for alternative imaginaries through attention to processes of representation at a potentially transformative moment for gender and sexual norms.

CREDITS

Director:
Ula Stöckl

Writer:
Ula Stöckl

Production Companies:
Ula Stöckl Filmproduktion
Thomas Mauch Filmproduktion

Produced by:
Ula Stöckl
Thomas Mauch

Cast:
Kristine de Loup (Anne)
Liane Hielscher (Katharina)
Heidi Stroh (Gabriele)
Elke Kummer (Magdalene)
Antje Ellermann (Kirke)
Jürgen Arndt (Stefan)
Alexander Kaempfe (Sascha)
Hartmut Kirste (Manfred)
Wolfgang von Ungern-Sternberg
    (Stefan's friend)

Cinematography:
Thomas Mauch
Dietrich Lohmann

Camera Assistant:
Jörg Schmidt-Reitwein

Film Editing:
Wolfgang Schacht

Assistance and Script:
Antje Ellermann

Lighting:
Dietmar Zander

Sound:
Folkhardt Prestin

Music:
Bob Degen
Fred Braceful
Manfred Eicher

Songs:
"Fleurs de Vacances," Marie Phillipine
    (Kristine de Loup)
"Die Katze hat 9 Leben," Erwin Halletz
    and Max Colpet

Runtime:
86 minutes

Soundmix:
Mono

Color:
Eastmancolor

Aspect Ratio:
2.35:1

Camera:
35mm, adapted for Techniscope

Negative Format:
35mm, 2-Perf

Process:
Techniscope

Printed Format:
35mm

Premiere:
October 12, 1968 (Mannheim International
    Film Festival)

NOTES

1 Laura Mulvey, "Visual Pleasure and Narrative Cinema," in *Visual and Other Pleasures* (Bloomington: Indiana University Press, 1989), 14. Mulvey wrote the essay in 1973; it was first published in 1975.

2 Qtd. in Bärbel Freund and Thomas Mauch, "Etwas über die Farben in *Neun Leben hat die Katze*," in *Ula Stöckl*, ed. Claudia Lenssen (Munich: edition text + kritik, 2019), 47. All translations from the German are my own.

3 In the film's opening credits, Kristine de Loup is listed pseudonymously as Marie Philippine.

4 Frieda Grafe, "Elektras Trauer: Ula Stöckls Film *Neun Leben hat die Katze* im Münchner Arri" (1974), rpt. in *Frauen und Film* 62 (2000): 101–2.

5 In 1977, the feminist film journal *Frauen und Film*, which was founded by Sander in 1973, devoted two special issues to the work of four established German women filmmakers, including Ula Stöckl, who did not come to film directly from the women's movement, in some cases because their entry into filmmaking preceded it. The journal's engagement with Stöckl's oeuvre represents the first attempt to situate it explicitly in relation to feminism; in an interview included in the issue, Stöckl also comments directly on her relation to the women's movement, pointing out that "I was always interested in women's themes, as the films themselves document, and the specific ways in which one ultimately becomes identified with a movement can be manifold." See Eva Hiller, Claudia Lenssen, and Gesine Strempel, "Gespräch mit Ula Stöckl," *Frauen und Film* 12, Special Issue, "Filmemacherinnen I" (June 1977): 8. The first detailed English-language analysis of Stöckl's oeuvre is offered by Marc Silberman, "How Women See Themselves," *New German Filmmakers: From Oberhausen through the 1970s*, ed. Klaus Phillips (New York: Frederick Ungar, 1984), 320–34.

6 Characteristic for its negative critical reception was Karl Korn's patronizing review in the *Frankfurter Allgemeine Zeitung*, which labeled the film "peinlich" (embarrassing); indicted its dual focus on emancipation and sexual liberation as uncritical; disapproved of its fashionable costumes and "sugarcoated color schemes"; and expressed relief that at least Katharina "achieved coitus" with a man in the course of the narrative. Karl Korn, "Trend zum Narzißmus," *FAZ* (11 Mar. 1969): 22. Peter M. Ladiges offers one of the few sympathetic critiques of the film from the period, emphasizing how its stylistic choices emerge from Stöckl's authorial vision as a woman filmmaker and concluding that "the result of Ula Stöckl's deliberations is that dominant society does not offer women any opportunity for fulfillment." Peter M. Ladiges, Rev. of *Neun Leben hat die Katze*, *Filmkritik* (1 Dec. 1968): 845.

7 On the distribution history of *Nine Lives*, see Hiller, Lenssen, and Strempel, "Gespräch mit Ula Stöckl," 6. Sources differ on the name of the distributor that Stöckl had contracted with and that later went bankrupt, but in interviews from the period Stöckl herself routinely refers to Eckelkamp.

8   *The Cat Has Nine Lives* is included on Disc 1 of the two-DVD set *Selbstbestimmt: Perspektiven von Filmemacherinnen* (Deutsche Kinemathek/Absolut Medien, 2019). The set is code-free and region-free, and all films included are subtitled in English.

9   See Toby Ashraf, "Verunsicherungen: Keine Ehe, keine Wahrheit, kein Junge: Queere Spuren im Werk von Ula Stöckl" (98), and Tatjana Turanskyj, "Fanpost" (37), in *Ula Stöckl*, ed. Lenssen. Turanskyj's films form direct intertextual relationships with *Nine Lives*, especially *Top Girl* (*Top Girl oder la deformation professionelle*, 2014). *Nine Lives* also serves as an important precursor for other recent feminist films from Germany, perhaps most notably Susanne Heinrich's *Aren't You Happy?* (*Das melancholische Mädchen*, 2019).

10 All quotes come from the official English subtitles on the DVD release. In some cases I have slightly modified the translations for clarity, as indicated by the addition of brackets.

11 Laura U. Marks, *The Skin of the Film: Intercultural Cinema, Embodiment, and the Senses* (Durham, NC: Duke University Press, 2000), 162; 138.

12 Grafe, "Elektras Trauer," 102.

13 Ula Stöckl, qtd. in Daniela Sannwald, *Von der Filmkrise zum Neuen Deutschen Film: Filmausbildung an der Hochschule für Gestaltung Ulm 1958–1968* (Berlin: Wissenschaftsverlag Volker Spiess, 1997), 103.

14 Claire Johnston, "Women's Cinema as Counter-Cinema," in *Notes on Women's Cinema* (London: Society for Education in Film and Television, 1973), 29.

15 Helke Sander, "aktionsrat zur befreiung der frauen," in *Die Neue Frauenbewegung in Deutschland: Abschied vom kleinen Unterschied—Eine Quellensammlung*, ed. Ilse Lenz (Wiesbaden: VS Verlag für Sozialwissenschaften, 2010), 61. A full English translation of the speech by Edith Hoshino Altbach is available as Helke Sander, "Speech by the Action Council for Women's Liberation," in *German Feminism: Readings in Politics and Literature* (Albany: State University of New York Press, 1984), 307–10.

16 Ula Stöckl, "Zuhause ist da, wo ich was verändern will," in *Wie haben Sie das gemacht? Aufzeichnungen zu Frauen und Filmen*, ed. Claudia Lenssen and Bettina Schoeller-Bouju (Marburg: Schüren, 2014), 102.

17 Stöckl discussed her relationship to the events of 1968 in a series of public interviews with Angelica Fenner, Barbara Mennel, and me at the University of Toronto in 2019.

18 Stöckl, "Zuhause ist da," 104.

19 "The Oberhausen Manifesto," in *West German Filmmakers on Film: Visions and Voices*, ed. Eric Rentschler (New York: Holmes & Meier, 1988), 2; Alexander Kluge, "What Do the 'Oberhauseners' Want? (1962)," in *West German Filmmakers on Film*, 12.

20 Kluge, "What Do the 'Oberhauseners' Want?," 12.

21 Claudia Lenssen, "Gruppenbild ohne Dame: Wo waren die Frauen am 28.2.1962?," in *Provokation der Wirklichkeit: Das Oberhausener Manifest und die Folgen*, ed. Ralph Eue and Lars Henrik Gass (Munich: edition text + kritik, 2012), 239.

22   See, for example, Claudia Lenssen, "Frauen-Rollen-Bilder 1966: Die Gleichzeitigkeit des Ungleichzeitigen," in *Deutschland 1966: Filmische Perspektiven in Ost und West*, ed. Connie Betz, Julia Pattis, and Rainer Rother (Berlin: Stiftung Deutsche Kinemathek, 2016), 151–63; Heide Schlüpmann, "'What Is Different Is Good': Women and Femininity in the Films of Alexander Kluge," *October* 46 (1988): 129–50; and John Urang, "Solitary Confinement: Reproduction and the Law in Kluge's 'Abschied von gestern,'" *New German Critique* 120 (2013): 111–35.

23   Caroline Rupprecht, "Post-War Iconographies: Wandering Women in Brecht, Duras, Kluge," *South Central Review* 26, no. 2 (2006): 37.

24   Urang, "Solitary Confinement," 113.

25   Stöckl, "Zuhause ist da," 103; 105.

26   Sabine Schöbel, Rev. of *Neun Leben hat die Katze*, *Frauen und Film* 62 (2000): 99.

27   Among the thirty-one students enrolled in the department between 1959 and 1968, there were ten women. See Peter Schubert and Monika Maus, eds., *Rückblicke: Die Abteilung Film-Institut für Filmgestaltung an der hfg Ulm 1960–1968* (Ulm: Club Off, 2012), 207.

28   Together with Helke Sander, Alemann founded the International Women's Film Seminar in West Berlin in 1973 to educate women about film history and empower them to seize the means of film production. In 1974, Alemann and Sander founded *Frauen und Film*, one of the earliest feminist film journals, which became a major site for the theorization of feminist aesthetics and women's film production.

29   Sannwald, *Von der Filmkrise*, 96.

30   Alexander Kluge, "Die Utopie Film," *Merkur* 18 (1964): 1140.

31   Edgar Reitz, "Utopie Kino," in *Liebe zu Kino: Utopien und Gedanken zum Autorenfilm 1962–1983* (Cologne: Verlag Köln, 1983), 18.

32   Report by Ula Stöckl in *Rückblicke*, ed. Schubert and Maus, 110.

33   Hiller, Lenssen, and Strempel, "Gespräch mit Ula Stöckl," 3.

34   Sabine Schöbel, "Erstmal lachen: Gespräch mit Ula Stöckl über *Neun Leben hat die Katze*," in *Frauen und Film* 68, Special Issue, "Aufbruch: Regisseurinnen der 60er" (2016): 118.

35   Frieda Grafe, Enno Patalas, and Wilhelm Roth, "Frau von dreißig Jahren: Gespräch mit Ula Stöckl," *Filmkritik* 2 (1969), rpt. in *Frauen und Film* 62 (2000): 100.

36   David Batchelor, "Chromophobia," in *Color: The Film Reader*, ed. Angela Dalle Vacche and Brian Price (New York: Routledge, 2006), 64.

37   On the Techniscope process, see Freund and Mauch, "Etwas über die Farben," esp. 51n2.

38   Claudia Gittel, "Kopie-Nachbildung: Davinci Resolve Workshop | *Neun Leben hat die Katze*," www.professional-production.de, Jan. 2016, accessed 29 Jan. 2020.

39   Freund and Mauch, "Etwas über die Farben," 50.

40   The English subtitle renders Anne's exclamation as "I'm pissed off"; what she says in French, however, is "Je m'emmerde," a colloquialism for "I'm bored stiff."

41   Ula Stöckl, "The Medea Myth in Contemporary Cinema," *Film Criticism* 10, no. 1 (1985): 47.

42   Roswitha Mueller, "Images in Balance," in *Gender and German Cinema: Feminist Interventions*, vol. 1, ed. Sandra Frieden et al. (Providence, RI: Berg, 1993), 65.

43   Uta Ganschow, "Wer bin ich? Drei Angebote aus der Mythologie," in *Ula Stöckl*, ed. Lenssen, 43.

44   Mueller, "Images in Balance," 65.

45   Schöbel, "Erstmal lachen," 115.

46   In addition to films featuring Antigone, Circe, and Medea, Stöckl also wrote and codirected, with Edgar Reitz, Alf Brustellin, and Nicos Perakis, *The Golden Thing* (*Das goldene Ding*, 1972), a retelling of the story of Jason and the Argonauts shot entirely with child actors. More recently, she has been working on the script for a film about Electra, which she hopes to shoot together with her students at the University of Central Florida. See Angelica Fenner and Hester Baer, "Feminist Filmmaking Before Feminism: An Interview with Ula Stöckl," *Feminist German Studies* 38, no. 1 (forthcoming 2022).

47   Sheila Johnson, "Modern Medea," in *Gender and German Cinema*, ed. Frieden et al., 93.

48   Johnston, "Women's Cinema as Counter-Cinema," 31.

49   Schöbel, "Erstmal lachen," 120.

50   Temby Caprio, "Women's Film Culture in the Sixties: Stars and Anti-Stars from *Papas Kino* to the New Wave," *Women in German Yearbook* 15 (2000): 217.

51   The soundtrack of *Nine Lives*, and the remarkable team that Stöckl assembled to create it, has sometimes been overlooked. The Austrian-born Halletz was a prolific composer of film scores in the 1950s and 1960s who also worked with major pop stars of the era, both in Germany and internationally. His cowriter on "The Cat Has Nine Lives," Max Colpet, was a Russian-born Jew who began his career as a cabaret artist in the Weimar Republic before fleeing Germany as a refugee from Hitler. Following an invitation from his friend Billy Wilder, Colpet eventually landed in Hollywood in the postwar period but returned to Germany in the 1950s and was particularly known for his German adaptation of the Pete Seeger antiwar song "Where Have All the Flowers Gone," recorded by Marlene Dietrich as "Sag mir, wo die Blumen sind." The score for *Nine Lives* was a collaboration of US-born jazz musicians Bob Degen and Fred Braceful with German-born producer Manfred Eicher, all significant figures in the postwar West German musical landscape. Eicher, in particular, went on to play a key role in the development of jazz, experimental, and avant-garde music through his record label ECM, founded in 1969.

52   Hiller, Lenssen, and Strempel, "Gespräch mit Ula Stöckl," 7.

53   Claudia Lenssen, "'When love goes right, nothing goes wrong . . .': '9 Leben hat die Katze'; 'Ein ganz perfektes Ehepaar'; 'Erikas Leidenschaft,'" *Frauen und Film* 12 (June 1977): 13.

54   Christina Gerhardt reads Anne as an Ophelia figure—owing to her association with both water and wildflowers and her white costumes—a resonance that emphasizes the pathologization of women's sexuality. Gerhardt, "On Liberated Women in an Un-Liberated Society: Ula Stöckl's *The Cat Has Nine Lives* (1968)," in *Women, Global Protest Movements, and Political Agency: Rethinking the Legacy of 1968*, ed. Sarah Colvin and Katharina Karcher (New York: Routledge, 2019), 69–81.

55   Caprio, "Women's Film Culture in the Sixties," 215.

56   For a discussion of this critical tendency, see Renate Möhrmann, *Die Frau mit der Kamera* (Munich: Carl Hanser Verlag, 1980), 37.

57   Elizabeth Grosz, *Time Travels: Feminism, Nature, Power* (Durham, NC: Duke University Press, 2005), 156–57.

58   Möhrmann, *Die Frau mit der Kamera*, 55.

59   Renate Fischetti and Christa Maerker, "'Frauenfilm ist eine Erfindung von Männern . . .': Gespräch mit Ula Stöckl," in Fischetti, *Das Neue Kino* (Frankfurt am Main: tende, 1992), 100–101.

60   Grosz, *Time Travels*, 155.

61   Stacy Alaimo, "The Naked Word: The Trans-Corporeal Ethics of the Protesting Body," *Women and Performance* 20, no. 1 (2010): 18.

62   Sarah Ensor, "Queer Fallout: Samuel R. Delaney and the Ecology of Cruising," *Environmental Humanities* 9, no. 1 (2017): 149.

63   Ensor, "Queer Fallout," 150.

64   Annie Sprinkle and Beth Stephens, "Ecosex Manifesto," http://sexecology.org/research-writing/ecosex-manifesto/, accessed 14 October 2020.

Printed in the United States
by Baker & Taylor Publisher Services